STOP
LEAVING LIFE
ON THE TABLE

DESIGN YOUR PATH AND
LIVE INTENTIONALLY

JOHN SALZWEDEL

For more information, email John@theCoach.vip.

ISBN: 979-8-89694-988-6 - Ebook
ISBN: 979-8-89694-989-3 - Paperback
ISBN: 979-8-89694-990-9 - Hardcover

Thank you for purchasing
STOP Leaving Life on the Table

As a thank you, I would like to offer you free access to my video summary of the material in the book. Just scan the QR code or go to:

https://jtslifecrafter.com/books/sllot_videosummary

Dedication

This book is dedicated to:

God. Who gave me life now and for eternity.

Mom and Dad. Who gave me a life to live and to learn.

Susan. Who gave my life "life,"
which I may not have found on my own.

Preface

You have a choice to make.
  Perhaps the easiest choice you will ever make.

Yet maybe the most difficult choice you'll ever make.

I'm talking about the choice of choosing your life over just letting life happen to you.

In regard to importance, it is the second most important decision you'll ever have to make. The first is your salvation. I'll talk about that in another book.

This could be the easiest choice to make in that I don't believe anyone who really looks at the two possibilities will have any trouble choosing the one they want.

This choice will determine how you approach every day of your life. Will you make it what you want or just let what happens happen?

Either way you're going to encounter problems; that's just part of life. But your mindset about life will make all the difference in how you respond to these challenges. You can make the choice to see every challenge as an opportunity to learn or as just another problem to endure.

A number of years ago, I had a revelation. I was sitting at my desk. The same desk I had been sitting at for nearly a quarter of a century. I had a good job. I worked for a good company. I worked alongside some great people. Everything was pretty darn good. But not really. Something wasn't right. I didn't know what. I had so much going for me, so what right did I have to complain? So, I was conflicted. I felt stuck. I was finding it harder to focus. The challenges of my job were no longer exciting me; "I'll do it later" was showing up too often, little things that should have just slid off my back made me angry, and the fun of getting out of bed and going to work was all but gone. I didn't know how to get unstuck, but I knew that I no longer wanted to do what I was doing.

Maybe I didn't know it then, but I had been sitting back for too long just letting life happen to me. I needed to make a change, but what and how? I didn't know who to talk to or what steps to take. I also had to consider my responsibilities. A steady paycheck with benefits was very helpful in paying the bills. I was also surrounded by people I cared about at work. Could I just step away?

If I did, where would I go? I had been in the insurance industry for more than two decades. What else was I suited for?

What would my family say? Would my friends think I was being rash or foolish?

I tried redesigning my job. I was in a position that allowed me to do that. This way I could stay with a good company, with the people I knew, and keep my paycheck and benefits. All strong reasons to stay in a job. I changed the things I was focused on, delegated what I could, and kept moving forward. But I was still stumbling in the dark.

So, I did what I've always done. I studied. I love learning, so I started reading books, listening to lectures, and watching videos. I learned from John Maxwell, Jim Rohn, Zig Ziglar, Stephen Covey, Dave Ramsey, Seth Godin, Simon Sinek, and many others. I read their books, listened to their speeches, and read the books that they read. I kept one question in my mind: "How do I redefine myself and my job?"

I joined the "John Maxwell Team" and did their training on coaching, speaking, and leading. I felt I could use that information in my current job to build up my team and make them better than they already were. It worked … for a while. Eventually, I began to feel the ache that something still wasn't right. So, I kept learning.

I got certified to teach the DISC personality profile (DISC is a personality inventory that teaches you about your tendencies when interacting with others.), and I got certified by the Ramsey organization to teach personal finance. I just kept learning.

Eventually, I figured out that I was not going to be able to carve what I felt I was supposed to be doing into the job I already had. I needed to design a plan to move on to something else. It was a tough decision as I had spent half my life with that company.

So, through trial and error—lots of error—I built a plan. It had to be a simple one; otherwise, I knew I wouldn't stick with it. That plan is built into this book.

I ended up leaving that job and starting a new business. I now spend my time writing, speaking, and coaching individuals. I am using my gifts in better alignment with my values and beliefs. And I love it! I even like getting out of bed in the morning.

And I have problems. All new ones. Things I didn't expect. This is hard work, but it is worth it. Designing my life didn't remove all my problems, but it helped me to enjoy tackling them more.

It is my hope that the information presented here is helpful to you and allows you to *build* and *live* the fulfilling and meaningful life you were designed to live.

That's why I'm here, and there will be others who will help you along the way. We will be there to shine the light on the path, give you tools to design and build your life, and to give you feedback when you need it. That's why we are here. But we're not going to do it for you.

We will help you because we have been there and know how tough it can be.

If you are ready to choose your life, then come along with me on a journey of discovering YOU. I believe that you can design and build that awesome life that you are meant to have. It won't be perfect. It won't be trouble-free. It won't always be easy. It will often be hard work. It will depend on your taking responsibility for your life. It will depend on your attitude. It will depend on your DESIGN.

Are you ready to unlock the joy and contentment of a life well lived?

If you are, then let's get to it.

Acknowledgements

No one takes on a project like this in a vacuum. I've had so many people help me write this both directly and indirectly. I know I will forget many people in my listing here. Please know that you have my thanks and that I will remember the role you played in its writing the next time I see you.

I would like to thank my Lord and Savior, Jesus Christ, without whom, my life would be meaningless.

Thank you to Susan for always being there. For caring for me even when I've been a jerk. For walking hand-in-hand with me for nearly 4 decades—so far. I'm looking forward to the next 4. It's gonna be fun!

Thank you to Mom and Dad. I appreciate all the sacrifices you made for me in my life. I've always known that you were there for me.

Thank you to Bettie Anne for being there for Dad. You never tried to replace Mom and you always gave your best to my dad and the rest of us.

Thank you to Zig and Jane for being the best in-laws a guy could want, for all you did in raising my bride, and for supporting us after we were married.

Thanks to Jeff and Jodi for all the important things you taught me, from time management to taking time to breathe to the importance of other people to the speed of a lemon twist. And also to Julie and Tim for taking care of the two of them over the years and for being a great additional brother and sister.

Thank you to my children, both blood and "adopted." Katrina, Jax, David, Matthew, Ivy, Dylan, Max, and Darrell, and my grandchildren, both blood and "adopted," Rowan, Holly, Maverick, and Gabriel. You all mean more to me than you know.

Thanks to my family at GRAND GENERAL. Much of what is in here, I learned when working side by side with you for those many years.

I have had more friends over the years than I could possibly name here. You know who you are. Thank you for being there to laugh with and to shine a light on to my path as I moved toward my purpose!

Thank you to my Toastmasters family, who have given me a safe place to practice my speech craft and a sounding board for many of the ideas in this book.

Thank you to my New Vision family, Brett, Martin, Kim, Kris, and Lisa. We learned a lot together, and you taught me a lot about looking at me.

Thank you to my family at St. Mark Lutheran Church. Through you I got to know my savior, met my wife, and learned a lot about serving. You've taught me a tremendous amount about leadership, giving, support, and friendship. A special shout-out to Scott Oostindie for his genuine joy of life and willingness to share it.

Thank you to the many speakers, writers, and authors who have influenced and taught me over the years, including Jim Rohn, John Maxwell, Zig Ziglar, Dave Ramsey, Simon Sinek, J.R.R. Tolkien, Stephen Lawhead, Hunter Charneski, Max Lucado, Dean Graziosi, Kurt Bubna, and more.

And a huge thank you to those brave souls who were willing to read this book before it got all shiny and pretty like the one you're about to read:

Dave Bouwkamp

Hunter Charneski

Randy Helder

Connie Howe

Jon Krueger

Jillian Murray

Dave Nelson

Marti Vieau

These people were open and honest about the good, the bad, and the confusing. Thank you for helping me clean it up.

Table of Contents

Section IV: DESIGN Application

Section V: Final Remarks

About the Book

I look at every book as a self-help book.

— Marc Maron

Is this another one of those self-help books?

The short answer is, '**Yes.**'

There is a reason there are so many self-help books available. It is because so many people are dissatisfied with some aspects of their life, and when it comes down to it, the only one who can change you is you. Self-help.

Each book out there will address different aspects of different problems in their own specific way. There are some great works that have been written. Many of which I have read myself. But I don't agree with all of them. The biggest difference I have with many of these books is the starting point. Many authors begin by examining an individual's current status. While I understand why they suggest it, I think we need to begin elsewhere.

Starting with our current status or our current problem limits our thinking (We will talk more about this in Section IV). We need to start with understanding ourselves. Not the surface us, or the temporary us. The real us.

I've written this book to take you through the life design process, in order. The process is meant to be applied to your overall life. However, it can be very helpful for those times when you are feeling stuck in just one area of your life.

This section will set the stage for you. I have always found it easier to understand someone when I know a little about them and their thought process.

I hope this will answer some of the questions that you have about the book and me before you even dig into it.

Why "Stop Leaving Life on the Table?"

People ask me why I chose such a strange name for my book. What does "Leaving Life on the Table" even mean?

If you work in business, you have probably heard the phrase, "We don't want to leave any money on the table." The idea behind this is that you want to make sure that you make every dime you can when you make a deal. If a customer is willing to pay $200, we don't want to sell for $150. If we do, we have just left $50 on the table.

When you craft a good business deal, you look at the needs of everyone involved and try to include them. If you can, you look at their wants as well as their needs. The more of each you can cover, the better the deal for everyone involved. A perfect deal leaves nothing on the table for either side. (Some would argue that a well-run business just looks at taking as much as they can without worrying about the other side of the transaction. It is a short-sighted viewpoint.)

But how many people leave *life* on the table? They settle for a life that shows up rather than the one they could have had with just a bit of self-evaluation, growth and intentionality. We only get one life here on earth. There is so much available to us, but can we stay curious enough to keep filling our lives with great experiences? How many people can we help? How much life can we "use up" by the time we're done? Or is our plan to "take it easy" as much as possible?

This doesn't mean that we must run with every wild idea that comes our way, though there may be times when that will be fun. Using up our life during our lifetime means taking the time to figure out what is important to us, what we are designed for, what our purpose is, and going after it with all of our energy. When we put everything into what is important to us, we're living our lives to the fullest.

When crafting our lives, we look at all of our relationships, our gifts, our talents, our passions, our values, our beliefs, and our opportunities. If we were to have these in alignment for our entire life, we would not be leaving any life on the table. As we all mess this up on occasion, we will leave some, but that's okay. We just keep learning and striving and doing our best.

The goal of this book is to help you leave as little on the table as possible.

You can do this.

Why this book now?

If you want to change the world,
pick up your pen and write.

— Martin Luther

Every day I look around and see miserable people. The number of individuals who are depressed keeps going up. Suicide has been on the rise for many years. It's a shame and it is preventable, or at least reducible.

Even people who are doing pretty well (as I was), feel there is something missing or not right in the lives they are living. It can be big or small.

I am not a psychologist. I don't have a medical degree, nor do I have any official training in social work.

What I do have is many years of working with people from all walks of life. From successful businesspeople to successful gardeners. From people who've gone bankrupt to those just trying to find their way. From people who live on the street or in the back seat of a car to those living in amazing mansions.

In my work with homeless or "street" people—those at the very lowest end of the financial spectrum—I have frequently seen them blaming the life that was handed to them. To be honest, many of them really seem to have received a bad hand. But the big problem is, they didn't have anyone to teach them that life can be different. What they have is all they know.

On the other end of the spectrum are those who have been handed everything. They have never known want, and they have never had to earn anything. They have never felt the warmth that comes from actually accomplishing something with their own hands. The problem is the same, no one has ever taught them that life could be any different.

We feel good when we accomplish things. We feel best when we are using our specific gifts and talents to fulfil our purpose. When we aren't doing this, we are leaving life on the table.

What I have found is that people are people. And people do better when they know what they are supposed to be doing and have a reason to get out of bed in the morning.

This book is meant to generate success ideas for anyone. It isn't focused on high-profile people. It is designed to give ideas to anyone and everyone, no matter what your title is or who calls you a friend. It is for the "Average Joe (or Jolene)."

I believe that every one of us has a purpose. We are given many gifts and talents. It is up to us to use them. I also believe that much of the depression and malaise that is so prevalent in our society arose because we have lost touch with ourselves. Our tendency is to look to others for everything. We all know people who have chosen to play the victim and blame someone else for their problems.

But that isn't you. You are here because you know life is tough, and you also know that if you want a better life, you have to make it. No one is going to give it to you.

So, I'm writing this book to encourage people to figure out what they (you) are called to do, and to give some exercises that can be turned into real-life actions.

Who should read this book?

Should is such a strong word. I think everyone could benefit from something in this book, but for me to say "should" is inappropriate or over-reaching.

I wrote this book for anyone who is trying to find their place in the world. I could have continued doing what I was doing in the insurance industry, but it no longer fit. I felt out of place.

I wrote this book for anyone who feels out of place where they are and wants to 'figure it out.' There isn't much here that you can't find elsewhere. It may be packaged a little differently. It is written by someone who has been through it and had to do a lot of the 'figuring out' on his own.

This was written by a regular person. Not a celebrity, not a doctor … certainly not AI. These are my words. I hope I have written it in a way that is easy to understand and simple (if not easy) to do.

I wrote this book for regular people who want more than they have. Who want to give more and receive more for their effort. I wrote this book for people who are willing to put in the work needed to really find who they are and how to use that information to the absolute fullest. I wrote this to the people who want to get to the end of life and say, *"I did some great things, some simple things, the things I was supposed to do. I did it well … and wow! That was fun!"*

If that sounds like you, then I wrote it for you.

Using this book

This book is for you. No one else. You spend a lot of your life thinking about what everyone else needs. That's good and you should do that. But you also need to spend time on yourself. Time to reflect, recenter, and refocus. That's how to use this book.

I don't want you to leave any life on the table. Use it all up.

The process described in this book is designed to help you learn who you are and how you can interact with others and to give you the skills you need to design the life you've always wanted, and then to get to work on it.

The information is here, but you must make it your own. Everyone's life is unique, and I can't spoon-feed you the answers. You will need to figure out how the concepts apply to you, especially when it comes to interacting with the people in your life.

This book is meant to get you thinking, but not to change methods that already work. If you have other ways to achieve the outcomes presented, and they work for you, then by all means use them. This book is meant to give you ideas. It won't solve all your problems.

The more of "you" that is in the solutions, the better they will work for you.

One last note on using this book. WRITE IN IT! Take notes, highlight, cross out … whatever. Any time the text causes you to think of something, write it down. There are many exercises to work on, do them! This book is meant to be a project for you.

I recommend that you get a notebook or journal of some sort and do your writing in a place that you can keep track of or revisit any time you wish. If I mention a form or worksheet, check the appendix and use it as a guideline for your journal or feel free to make copies to write on. You can also go to my website and download printable pdf's. www.theCoach.vip/ SLLOT .

My Glasses

We all see the world in a unique way. Through our own "glasses." The lenses of our glasses were formed by the place we were born, our parents, the people around us, and the things we have read and heard. Everything that formed us also formed how we see things.

Though I believe that everything in this book can be applied to anyone's worldview, there is one element of "my glasses" that I thought I should tell you about as it greatly affects everything I do and say. You should know this so that you know how to make any adjustments you need to make.

I am a Christian. It is the single most important role I play and it defines how I relate to people and to God. I believe that God created each of us, individually with inherent value and a specific purpose that will expand as we grow. He created us to worship Him (I use the masculine pronoun out of tradition, but we, whether we are male or female, are created in His image).

Through my *glasses* I believe that God wants us to use our gifts and talents with pride serving Him and our fellow humans. We should treat other people in the way we wish to be treated (Golden Rule). Interestingly, most, if not all, of the major religions in the world contain some version of the Golden Rule.[1]

---

[1]   www.goldenruleproject.org/formulations lists hundreds of versions of the Golden Rule

Buddhism: "Hurt not others in ways that you yourself would find painful."

Christianity: "Do to others as you would have them do to you."

Confucianism: "Do not do to others what you do not want them to do to you."

Hinduism: "One should not behave toward others in a way which is disagreeable to oneself."

Humanist: "Don't do things you wouldn't want to have done to you."

Islam: "None of you truly believes until he wishes for others that which he wishes for himself."

Judaism: "What is hateful to you, do not do to your fellow man."

We should also do all that we can to show people the way to everlasting life. I believe the only way to receive eternal life is by accepting the free gift of salvation through faith in Jesus, true God and true man, who suffered and died on our behalf, and then rose again.

You will see this bias throughout the book. I won't disguise it. As I do not know what you believe, you may have to do some translation to fit your worldview.

If you are interested in what it means to be a Christian and what it takes to become one. Reach out to me at my website, www.theCoach.vip/Christianity.

Introduction

If you spend your entire day "killing time,"
time will start killing you.

— Warning from the author

L ife is Tough. There is no way around it. It's just tough. We scratch and claw our way through, trying to survive, or perhaps trying to be the one who dies with the most toys. We have an annoying buzzer wake us up every morning so that we can go to a job that we may dread. Maybe we're even trying to impress people we don't really even like. I hope that it isn't you, but it has been me on occasion.

We do it to pay the bills or be the person we were told to be. Like it or not, no matter what anyone tries to tell you, sometimes you have to do a job you don't enjoy because you have responsibilities to meet. That's just the way it is, and it is a good thing. It means you have your priorities in order. But what do we do when it stops feeling like a good thing?

We've all heard those motivational speakers who talk about how they fell off a mountain, broke 3 legs and an ear on the way down. They somehow overcame that 4-year recovery to run two marathons and an Ironman triathlon in one weekend. It's very inspiring for a bit, and I give them credit for having done it. The problem is that I haven't had that huge obstacle to overcome. No huge traumas, or diseases. Sure, I've had bad things happen, we all have, but I feel guilty about being depressed when things are actually not that bad—especially when I think of all they and others have overcome.

However, that guilt is unwarranted, and if you have felt it, let yourself off the hook. Problems are problems whether they are big or small. They wear us down whether they are debilitating or just annoying. It is okay to be sad or angered at the little things. Sometimes you just need to sit in the corner and cry for a little while. If that's where you are, then do that. Put this book down, find a quiet spot and let it all out. Do some crying or hit a punching bag. Get that sadness or anger out of you. But don't stay sitting in your corner. Keep it short and then get back to living. Because whether you have average Joe problems or Gandhi-sized problems, there is a way through them. And you will have the knowledge to find it.

In this book we will discuss how you can discover the life that you've always wanted and feel you were meant to have. And we will go through a process to help you build it. To be clear, you will design it, and then as time goes by you will have to change your design, because your world will change and so must your life design. That's also a good thing because it means you are growing.

Getting the most out of your life requires putting the most into your life. Other than God's grace, we don't get anything for nothing.

Each of us has the responsibility to find out why we're here— what we're supposed to be doing in this life. When we do that, we find joy and contentment that we can't get any other way.

Notice I didn't say it would be easy—nor did I say you'll never work a day in your life. It doesn't happen that way.

The notion of using your gifts and talents in doing something you love to do has nothing to do with being easy or fun.

I don't think there is anyone who would disagree with me that Mother Theresa was doing what she was called to do and that she was good at it. I also don't think anyone would disagree with me that she worked very hard.

But she loved what she was doing. She had the contentment and the exhilaration that comes from working hard, doing your best, and seeing the fruits of a life well spent.

What about you?

I'm going to make a couple of assumptions about you. They might be wrong, but I'm going to make them anyway.

I am assuming:

1) You picked up this book because you want to see if I have any ideas you could use to improve how you are living your life. (I might, but you will have to make them your own.)

2) You aren't afraid to work. You wouldn't have picked up a book with this description (or written by me, if you know me) if you were looking for cheap or easy success.

3) You understand that I won't list every example or scenario and that you will have to translate this information to fit your life.

4) You will take responsibility for your life. You won't pass the blame to anyone else when you mess up or when something doesn't work.

Everything I will present in this book is based on what I've learned by making lots of mistakes. Even today I am still making some of the mistakes that already taught me lessons. I'm sure this will continue for the rest of my life.

I wrote this book out of my life experiences and what I've learned by talking and listening to others who have also had some success in designing the life they want. Like me, the book isn't perfect, but I hope it will be helpful to you.

So, if you're ready to get building, then turn the page to start figuring out who you really are.

Section I
Who Are You?

Knowing yourself is the beginning of wisdom.

— Aristotle

Be yourself; everyone else is already taken.

— Oscar Wilde

Before you can design your life, before you can feel any contentment, before you can consistently make your right decisions, you have to know who you are.

I'm not talking about the surface you or the 'you' that people tell you to be. I'm talking about the real, deep-down, inside, *you*. Ideally, these are the same. For most of us, they aren't.

If you want to live your best life, and don't want to leave any life on the table, then you must know *you*. A strong knowledge of what you believe, what you stand for, and what lines can and can't be crossed will help you later in this book (and in your day-to-day life) as we discuss your roles, goals, and actions.

Relation to Self

When we think about our relationship with ourselves, we have to start with our beliefs, values, and principles. These are the things we know to be true. They do not change often; some never do. Our values and beliefs determine everything about us, what's important and for what we stand. If we understand them clearly and create our principles based on them, then our principles will guide all our actions and help us to make decisions before they even arise. Decisions can be tough "in the moment" because we can get stuck in the emotions of the event or the condition of our attitude at that moment. When we have a clear set of values and beliefs, we can make decisions from our unmoving center, rather than our frequently moving emotional state.

If we have a clear definition of what's right and wrong ahead of time, this will help us to avoid mistakes. We *know* what we should be doing without the emotions, or social pressures, or financial pressures that show up in real life. It is a lot easier to stand up for what you believe in when you know clearly what that is.

The goal is to keep all our actions consistent with our beliefs. When we don't do this, our stress increases. This is because we know we are wrong. We are sure of this because we have defined what is right and wrong.

I had mentioned previously that for me, my relationship to God is the source of my values. For those of you who do not have that belief in God, you will have to determine the source of your values. Is it society? Is it your family and friends? Is it social media? Is it the government? Is it science? To understand yourself, you need to know this.

As you spend time determining what is important to you, what you stand for, what you'll accept, and what you won't accept, you will get to know yourself a little bit better and maybe understand your decisions a little bit more. It isn't a quick process. Don't rush it. It will take years for you to have a full understanding of yourself. Since you are changing constantly, these beliefs and values will change too, but not as quickly as other things do.

In this book, I will use myself as an example a lot. It is because I know me better than I know anyone else.

When we begin examining our beliefs and values, we start with the easy ones. The beliefs and values that pop into your head immediately. Here are some of mine, yours will likely be different:

I believe in God. I believe in the Christian Triune God. The words in the Bible are the source of my beliefs and ethics.

I believe that integrity is one of the few things I can actually control in my life. I should do what I say. I should be honest. An honest day's work for an honest day's pay. Follow my rules, even when no one is watching.

I believe that I am responsible for my own actions. I can't control what happens to me, but I can control how I respond to what happens to me.

I believe there is always a solution. If there isn't a solution, then it isn't a problem; it's just a fact. Gravity may get in my way, but it can't be "solved."

I can solve how I interact with gravity if I need to. Have you ever seen an airplane fly?

I believe there is always something new to learn. I will never stop.

I believe that I should treat others the same way I wish to be treated.

Getting to know yourself is simple, but it isn't easy. This section is a tough one, but it is the basis for everything else we talk about. Really be honest with yourself as you go through. It's all for you, you won't need to share it with anyone. Fight through it because your life is worth it.

So, what do you believe? Let's find out.

Chapter 1
Beliefs, Values, and Principles

*My son, do not lose sight of these—keep sound
wisdom and discretion, and they will be life for
your soul and adornment for your neck.*

— Proverbs 3:21–22 ESV

To thine own self be true.

— William Shakespeare, *Hamlet*, Act I, Scene 3

Belief: Whatever we believe to be true

Value (Core Value): Those beliefs which we find to be
important and desirable

Principles: Our rules that stem from our core values

*We don't see the world as it is,
we see the world as we are.*

— Stephen Covey, *The Seven Habits of Highly Effective People*

Beliefs

How do you see the world?

It is our beliefs that determine who "we are" and, therefore, how we see the world.

A group of blind men heard that a strange animal, called an elephant, had been brought to the town, but none of them were aware of its shape and form. Out of curiosity, they said: "We must inspect and know it by touch, of which we are capable." So, they sought it out, and when they found it, they groped about it. The first person, whose hand landed on the trunk, said, "This being is like a thick snake." For another one whose hand reached its ear, it seemed like a kind of fan. As for another person, whose hand was upon its leg, said, "The elephant is a pillar like a tree-trunk." The blind man who placed his hand upon its side said, "The elephant, is a wall." Another who felt its tail described it as a rope. The last felt its tusk, stating, "The elephant is that which is hard, smooth, and like a spear."[2]

Our view of the world depends upon our experiences. Our view may be right, or it may be wrong, or it may be completely subjective, not having a right or wrong. The important part is to be aware that there are very few things in life of which we have a true picture. How we see something may be different than how someone else sees it. This is why I spent so much time explaining my glasses early on.

---

[2]   This story appears in ancient Jain, Hindu and Buddhist texts (circa 500 B.C.)

Some examples of beliefs.

These are some of my beliefs. Yours will, and should be, different:

- God created everything
- Jesus lived and died for us
- All people have value
- There is a solution to every problem
- We all have many roles to fill, and we should do so to the best of our abilities.
- Education should never end
- Integrity is one of the few things about us over which we have complete control
- We can't change what happens to us, but we can control how we react to what happens to us

What we are doing here is true soul-searching. A lot of what you will find in this process has been with you most of your life. These tend to be the ideals taught to you by your parents or other important people in your life. They may also come from friends or your own evaluation of what is going on in the world around you.

The biggest danger at this moment of discovery is writing things down, in stone, too quickly. Yes, you do need to be writing these down, but so much of what we "believe" is because we are told to believe it.

Don't do that. It is fine if you start exploring a belief because someone told you to, but don't believe it because they said you should. When you begin examining your beliefs, write them down in pencil. Just get the basic idea written, then go through and examine it—think about every word. And make adjustments as you need to.

It might look something like this:

I believe that God created the world.

Then,

I believe the world was designed and created by God.

Then,

I believe that God loves us and designed and created a physical place for us to live.

Keep working on it until the words say what you want them to. You're trying to put words to the things that you truly believe.

I chose the belief above as one to write down because it is important to who I am and hopefully, how I act. That is where we move from beliefs to values. Core Values are those beliefs that are important to us and should control how we act.

Values

In the previous section I listed many beliefs, and then I chose one that is important to me. As you go through this exercise, you will actually choose several of your beliefs which are important to you and dig into them a little bit more. These will be statements of your values.

Here is how I expanded on the belief about God creating the world:

> **God created the world**, so it is His, and I am here to enjoy it and take care of it.
>
> **God loves us.** This tells me why God created the world. He wanted us to have a physical place where we could be physical beings and enjoy all that life has to offer, and where He can enjoy us as well.
>
> **God designed the world.** It wasn't just thrown together willy-nilly. God made the universe the way that He made it—on purpose. We can see a glimpse of the grandeur of God through the amazing intricacies of His creation.

Another Core Value for me is integrity. I believe in being completely honest, in telling the full truth, not just the portion of the truth that will get the result I want. It is doing what I say I will do, taking responsibility for those things which I do, as well as those things I don't do and should have done. I've heard it said that integrity is who you are when no one is watching. It is acting in the way that you believe is right, even if you know that no one will ever find out. I also believe it is in my control. For me:

There is an absolute source of right and wrong. I believe that God is the source of right and wrong.

God does not change. Right and wrong is not determined by circumstances or how I am feeling.

God gave us free will. I can choose whether I wish to follow God's description of right and wrong. Others also have free will and can make that same choice.

I want to do what is right. I want to do right because I want to please God and because I believe that what God says is right will lead us to the best life we can have.

The world is bigger than me. I can choose what I do, how I react. I cannot change what anyone else does or what happens to me.

Understanding these beliefs and what they mean to us is the reason we are writing them down. When we have our values, then we use those to create our own rules. That is how we stay true to ourselves day by day.

Principles

Sometimes you're wrong.

— Gibbs' Rules, #51

My favorite display of principles in pop culture is Gibbs' Rules from the television show *NCIS*. These are the rules of life that

Leroy Jethro Gibbs tried to live by and teach to his team. In the series, we learn a little bit about where the rules come from, but in season 7, episode 24, we see the creation of my favorite rule: #51, "Sometimes you're wrong." No one is perfect.

Principles are created when we take the values we developed and use them to determine or "control" our actions and reactions. Principles are the curbs to our behavior ... stay within the lines.

> **God created the world**, so it is His, and I am here to enjoy it and take care of it.

A principle from this value might be that the world is God's. So, I won't litter. It is my job to try to keep it looking as good or even better than the day I got here.

Belief	Value (Core Value)	Principle
What we believe to be true	*An important or desirable belief*	*Our personal rule related to the value*
God created the world	I should take care of the world	I won't litter
God is the source of right and wrong	I will have integrity	I will choose to do right, whether anyone is looking or not

Have you ever heard of geocaching? It is a lot of fun and exercises your body and your brain. In essence, it is a worldwide treasure hunt, where the treasure is "finding the cache." Typically, it is a small box containing a piece of paper to sign your name. Maybe a few trinkets to trade. There are millions of them located worldwide. They can be in the middle of a parking lot or the middle of a forest. And the people who hide them are very creative.

One reason I like geocaching is CITO: this means Cache In-Trash Out. When we're geocaching, it is expected that we will pick up any trash we may find lying around. It is also expected that we won't litter or damage anything. Leave only footprints. This expectation is consistent with my value of taking care of the world and my principle of not littering.

Principles are what give life to our values and beliefs. They guide our actions. They help us to know how we believe we are to behave.

Whether we believe in absolutes or not, when we are not living in alignment with our principles, we can tell. We don't feel at peace. We know we are wrong. When our actions do match our beliefs (in alignment) we can tell that too. We feel the peace, like everything is in line. We are energized because we are actually BEING the person we want to be.

If you don't stand for something—you will fall for anything.[3]

Have you ever had someone present an idea to you on something that you've never even thought about? In that situation, our tendency is to trust that the person knows what they are talking about—because they know more than we do; for example, we tend to give authors the benefit of the doubt. I

---

[3]   There is dispute as to the origin of this phrase. Suffice to say, it isn't my creation.

wrote a book, so I must know what I'm talking about. Maybe I do, but make sure it makes sense to you; don't just believe me.

Perhaps we just go along because we haven't thought about it. More than once in my life this has led me to a moment of asking: "What was I thinking? That isn't me." Those moments hurt. They hurt because I know that I failed myself (in that moment, not permanently).

The clearer we set our principles, our guides, our curbs, the less likely it will be for this to happen. Take your time doing this. Remember, just like Gibbs, you will add and adjust principles as you go through life. Don't be afraid of that. You will be doing it because you are growing.

A number of years ago, my wife and I were training for our first black belts in karate. We were both scheduled to test on the same day. Our sensei asked how I would feel about having my wife as my testing partner. I refused. He asked me what I would do if he set it up anyway. I told him that I would not get my black belt.

I had been working toward my black belt for many years. I can't even begin to quantify the hours I put in training. But the karate black belt test is not a "hands off" affair. We left these tests bruised and sometimes bloodied and even broken.

I was ready for that. And even though exercise and the amount of work I put into karate was important to me, I will never raise a hand to my wife. Never. It is one of my very highest principles. He had me test with a man about my size with similar skills. He and I actually tested together several times in the future.

I could very quickly make that decision because I knew which priorities were highest for me.

Step-by-Step

I recommend having a notebook or journal where you can track all your brainstorming and plans.

Worksheets are available in the appendix or at www.theCoach.vip/SLLOT

1. Write out as many beliefs as you can.

2. Carefully choose the best words to describe those beliefs.

3. Choose which beliefs are most important to your life, these are values.

4. Write down some principles that come from the values.

Chapter 2

Why You Exist: Finding Your Purpose

The proper function of man is to live, not to exist. I shall not waste my days in trying to prolong them. I shall use my time.

— Jack London

Your passion is for you. Your purpose is for others.

— Jay Shetty, *Think Like a Monk*

A recent survey asked people, "**If you could ask God one question, and get an immediate answer, what would you ask?**"

I would have guessed that the question would have something to do with eternity. It didn't. The number one question people would ask is, "**Why am I here?**" or "**What is my purpose?**"

The good news is: we can find our purpose even if we don't audibly get an answer from God to the question. The first place to start in finding your purpose is to understand that it will not conflict with your beliefs and values. That is one of the reasons it is important to nail down your standards before you dive into purpose. If you believe your purpose is in violation of your values, then one of them is wrong. Either you have written down a value wrong, or you have determined your purpose wrong. You will not have a purpose that contradicts who you really are. Situations such as that are a major cause of stress and anxiety in our lives.

I've heard the question before, "If you had all the money in the world and you knew that you couldn't fail, what would you do?" This is meant to be a question to help you find your purpose. What I have found is that it is better to ask, "If I had all the money in the world and I knew I could still fail, what would I do because it's important enough to take the risk?" I believe this shows us better where our heart lies.

I mentioned earlier in this book how much I had struggled with this question a few years back. I've actually struggled with this a number of times in my life. Since I think this is an important question, I am going to dig pretty deep into my own examples.

According to research conducted by Larissa Rainey in 2014, up to 91% of people are confused as to who they are and what they are supposed to be doing in life.[4] If you assume that number hasn't changed (My guess is that it has gone up.), that means that over 238 million people aged 18 and over in the United States don't know their purpose.

If it was just those people who don't have some religious affiliation that were feeling this, then I would say that the lack of that tradition was the reason. But that isn't the case. I know many people in numerous religions who are just as confused on the question.

---

[4] www.psychologytoday.com/us/blog/the-regret-free-life/202502/americas-purpose-crisis

I believe the greatest cause of this is twofold.

First, we have so many more options than we have had in the past—and they fly at us constantly. It's like shopping for chips at the grocery store. It was easy many years ago when your choice was plain chips or ridged chips. Have you looked at the chip aisle, yes, the entire aisle, at a grocery store? So many choices.

The same is true of careers. Eighty years ago, if you wanted to be a medical doctor, it was pretty much a choice of being a doctor for people or for animals. Maybe a few specialties.

But today, if you just look at the choices for being an animal doctor ... Do you want to take care of farm animals or domestic pets? How about exotics or maybe emergency veterinarian medicine? A dog specialist? Parrots? Amphibians? Snakes or fish or ...?

And if we like bits and pieces of twelve different jobs/careers ... How can we decide?

When I was in college, I had at least four different majors in my first two years. Engineering, Foreign Languages, Business, Pre-seminary, and probably several others I can't even remember anymore. I was good at a lot of things, but nothing I had found really fired me up into a desire for a lifelong career. So, I left college for a year.

I joined a music ministry team from Lutheran Youth Encounter, a great organization which, unfortunately, no longer sends out teams. For 14 months, my team (6 "random" people thrown together) traveled in a van through the central United States and then to Australia and Papua New Guinea, where we traveled by every means imaginable.

We traveled to established churches and events, using music, skits, and educational programs to support and build up the members and friends of these congregations and groups.

It was a fantastic experience, and I think we did some good. For me personally, it got me out of my sheltered Midwest life and showed me a wide world of differences and opportunities. It gave me a chance to talk to many people and to experience many different tasks and jobs.

Interestingly, when I finished those 14 months, my desire was to move into the business world, even though I did very little of that during my time on the road.

I got a bachelor's degree in business, a master's degree in management, and then bounced from job to job until I ended up in the insurance industry, working for my dad.

My dad always said that he ended up in insurance to pay the bills until he found something better. Sixty years later, he was still looking.

For me, I got into insurance the same way. The industry was very good to me and I learned a lot and made a lot of friends. It was 20 years into that career when I started feeling that something wasn't right. By this time, I was the CEO of a national wholesaler and was meeting with other CEO's and industry leaders. I started to see in them a passion and desire for the industry that I just didn't feel. I tried to find ways to generate that passion but was unable to do so.

As I have mentioned before, I started reading everything I could find, watching and listening to speeches, attending seminars … anything I could think of to find my way out of this funk in which I found myself.

It became clear that the first thing I needed to do was to take the time necessary to figure out who I was, what I stood for, and what was important to me. Which brings us to reason number two.

The second reason for the great amount of unrest and uncertainty about purpose is due to the busyness of our world today and the speed at which everything moves. We do not, maybe cannot, take the time we need to figure out who we really are. We don't stop and think; we don't evaluate what is around us. We look at people on TV and social media and assume they have it all figured out. They don't. They're making it up as they go along. They are taking the easy answers that feel good at the moment but have no lasting meaning. Not everyone, of course, but the vast majority. And even if they do have it figured out, *they aren't you!*

Finding what is truly important to you, what you were designed to be, takes some work, but if you figure it out and use that information, it makes all the difference.

Are you ready to dig in?

Finding your purpose comes down to asking yourself, and others, a lot of questions, and taking the time to find the central point of the answers. Here are some examples of questions to ask yourself:

What tasks energize me?

What am I good at?

What roles make me smile?

What makes me cry or breaks my heart?

What do I truly see as the single greatest need in the world?

What would I want said in my eulogy?

If I overheard someone talking about me, what would I hope to hear?

Who do I admire and why?

Who do I despise and why?

Who are the most important people in my life? How can I best serve them?

What are my most important activities and why?

What makes me smile all day?

Is there something that I feel, if I worked at it, I could be the best in the world?

What comes naturally to me?

How do I best serve people in general?

What do I want?

For what has life prepared me?

And finally, any other questions that you think help you understand yourself a little more.

Let's look at these questions a little closer and see what we're looking for and what we'll do with the information.

What tasks energize me?

This was the biggest thing that was missing in my life when I was considering the industry change. Getting up in the morning for work was something I did because I had to, not because I wanted to. On the weekends, I'd get up early and do a lot ... during the week, it was so much harder. How I was spending my time during the week did not give me energy, it took energy.

The idea here is that the things that are important to you are far more likely to give you energy than anything else. They might completely wear us out, but you can't help but keep going. The energy comes from the purpose. Whatever you are doing is important, for whatever reason, so your mind tells your body "just one more." And then repeats it again and again.

What am I good at?

This is the one that makes me smile because we get to do some internal bragging. Our society doesn't like us talking about how good we are at something. But give yourself permission to do it here. What are you really good at? There is a reason that you are good at it, and there is a very good chance that your purpose is related to the things you are good at.

For me, I'm very good at finding options and solutions. I am far better at listening than I used to be.

There may be something that you love to do—but you're just not very good at it. Don't stop doing it! Either practice until you are good at it, or you call it a hobby and enjoy it any time you wish just for the fun of doing it.

What roles make me smile?

We haven't really talked about roles yet in the book. It's coming up in Chapter 3. Roles are the different parts we play in life.

This could be spouse, parent, child, sibling, boss, church member. Whatever you do.

When you figure out the many different roles you hold, consider which ones make you smile and which you feel are a drudgery. You don't necessarily get to "remove yourself" from the drudgery roles; sometimes you just gotta do what you gotta do. But knowing what they are helps you to understand *you*.

The ones that you enjoy the most will be important in your evaluation of purpose and also your setting of priorities.

What makes me cry or breaks my heart?

Did you ever see something happen somewhere, maybe even in a movie or in a book, and you just wanted to cry for the situation? This tug at your heartstrings highlights an aspect of your purpose. If it wasn't important, you wouldn't care. If you hurt, then you care, and it is important to you.

There is an episode of M*A*S*H that brings a tear to my eye every time I see it. It is called "Death Takes a Holiday" (Season 9, Episode 5). I don't get emotional for the reason I think most people would expect.

During the episode, they are collecting food for a party for the orphans in the area. Charles wouldn't contribute, though he certainly had the means. Everyone was very hard on him because he had received lots of packages marked perishable but was unwilling to donate. However, his family had a tradition of giving gifts under the condition that it must remain anonymous. He had already given all of the packages to the orphans but not told anyone. At the very end, Charles was sitting alone, having a cognac, feeling very misunderstood, and knowing he couldn't explain things. Max came in, brought him some food, and had this conversation:[5]

Cpl. Maxwell Q. Klinger: [*wheels an assortment of dishes into the Swamp*] Ah, Major Winchester, the party of one. Dinner is served.

Major Charles Winchester: What is this?

Klinger: Well, let's see. For your appetizer, the last of the macadamias, followed by a mixed grill of Lebanese salami, sugar-cured ham, pigs' feet, and hog jowls. We have seconds on those. Sorry, sir, no smoked oysters. I just smoked the last one. Ah, and for dessert ... Frisco fudge and nutty fruitcake.

Winchester: All laced with hemlock, I'm sure.

Klinger: Sorry, sir. No hemlock. But I can get you some ketchup.

Winchester: And what, pray tell, is the catch of the day?

Klinger: Oh, just one catch, Major. The source of this Christmas dinner must remain anonymous. It's an old family tradition.

[*smiles at Charles, indicating that he knows about his very generous deed for the orphanage*]

Winchester: Thank you, Max.

Klinger: Merry Christmas, Charles.

---

[5]   "Death Takes a Holiday" 1980. M*A*S*H, season 9, episode 5, Twentieth Century Fox Home Entertainment LLC, 2005, disc 1.

Even typing this gets my eyes watering. Someone understands Charles. Even if it is only one person, for Charles, that is enough.

What do I truly see as the single greatest need in the world?

The world is messed up. No question about it. It is a very beautiful place and has some wonderful people in it. Even the most wonderful person messes up on occasion. That's just the way it is.

But is there one idea or concept that you feel would make all the difference? If we, as a species, did one thing better, it would change the world? What would that thing be?

This question helps to dig into what is important to you. That will give us clues to your purpose.

Perhaps it is, "if we made sure everyone had enough food, everything would be great." That's a great goal, and many people are driven by it. It is something we need to fix, but it isn't my passion. If it is yours, please do it. It would be so awesome if everyone had enough food.

For me, I believe the single thing that would change the world the most is acceptance of the value of people around us, and ourselves. The media and advertising are constantly telling us that we're not good enough, and social media is constantly showing us how glorious others are but we're not, and television and movies typically will make fun of regular people who are trying to do their best.

If we change how we see and interact with other people, the entire world will change. Everyone would probably be fed, too.

What would I want said in my eulogy?

Someday you're going to die. I'm sorry to be the bearer of bad news if you were hoping for otherwise. (If you're interested in learning about how to live after you die, there is a way. Send me a note.)

This is a time you get to think about the perfect you. Imagine it is some time down the road. You can choose how long but make it at least 20 years from now. You've just died. Through some miracle, you are able to float above your funeral and listen to the proceedings. What do you hope you will hear? Do you want to hear you were a great athlete? That you worked hard to feed the world? That you listened when others spoke? That you were always there with the hug someone needed? That you were the best computer programmer ever? That you could make a slide-rule sing?[6]

You won't need to share this with anyone, so be honest with yourself. You've lived an amazing life … What did you accomplish? And don't worry if the accomplishments seem huge or tiny. Either one can still be important to you and many others around you.

I would recommend you actually write out your eulogy. Choose your words carefully just as you would if you were asked to write the eulogy for someone important to you.

---

[6]   A slide rule is basically an analog calculator. It looks like a ruler with a center portion that slides. It can do basic math such as multiplication, division, logarithms, trigonometry and more. It was invented 400 years ago.

This can be difficult, and maybe a little sad. It can also be energizing and can help you to see the big picture of who you want to be and what is truly important to you. These things won't all be earth-shattering, but some of them might be.

For me, I think the one thing that I would most want to hear is "He was always there for me and made me feel important."

If I overheard someone talking about me, what would I hope to hear?

Have you ever received a "butt-dial" on your phone? I got one once, when I missed the call and the caller went into my voicemail, and stayed there for nearly 20 minutes. The caller was the sales representative for one of the companies that wanted me to do business with them. He was at a bar and his mouth runneth over. Be careful of your phone and your mouth!

That's all I've got to say about that.

— Forrest Gump

In this exercise, you are going to imagine that this happened to you, and the caller was a friend of yours, or maybe a co-worker. Someone who knows you pretty well. What do you hope you hear in the conversation? This is very similar to the eulogy question, but maybe a bit more personal. The eulogy is being said in front of lots of people; this is more private.

When they discuss you in this way—who do you hope they say you are?

Who do I admire and why?

We tend to admire the people who hold ideals similar to our own. By looking at who you admire, you can get an idea of who you want to be. We can and should admire people for specific things even if we don't admire them for everything. (Remember, no one is perfect.)

So, we pick some people we admire. We then ask ourselves: What it is about them that we admire? But we don't stop there. We must then ask: Why is this important to us?

Here is an example. I admire my dad for his ethic of hard work and also his acceptance of making mistakes. He once said, "If you aren't making mistakes, then you aren't learning anything."

I think both of those ideas are important.

Hard work is important because it will get us where we want to go. We need to earn—work for—our best life. I have trouble coming up with examples of people who were *given* everything they wanted and then made a real contribution to society or even to their family or to themselves. If they are given something for nothing, they don't tend to appreciate it, and they don't do anything good with it. If it is earned, then it means something. It lets you feel good about what you've done and what you've created. More importantly, it gives you the desire to help others to earn what they want.

Making mistakes is important too. Nothing grows without taking chances.

> *A ship is safe in harbor,*
> *but that's not what ships are for.*
>
> — John A. Shedd

We must go out on the ocean if we want to see the world and learn what there is to learn. And when we do so, we will make mistakes. Through those mistakes, we learn, and this will change us. Our priorities and goals may change with every step we take.

Who do I despise and why?

In Sunday School we were taught not to hate anyone. In this book I have mentioned that everyone has value. I truly believe that, so how can I even ask who I despise? It is because it does a very nice job of highlighting our purpose. If we hate someone, or more correctly, hate their actions, it is usually because it is contrary to one or more of our values.

For me, who I hate the most is not a specific person. It is when people forget there are other people in the world and that they matter too. It becomes very obvious in very small ways.

Cutting people off in traffic because where you are going is more important.

Running a red light because the seven seconds you're going to save is worth risking someone's life.

Interrupting a conversation someone is having because what you are going to say is more valuable.

I must stop myself on this list of pet peeves. I could go on for far too long, and you didn't buy this book to hear my whining. I'm listing a few of these as examples of what I hate.

The reason that I hate it, the why, is that when we do this to someone, we are telling them that they are not as important as we are; that our need or want must come first.

No matter who you are, or who they are, we all have an inherent value. We all matter. The self-important attitude described above directly conflicts with my belief that ALL people have value.

Who are the most important people in my life? How can I best serve them?

We will delve into this question a lot in our chapter on Priorities (Chapter 4). But for this portion, just think about the one or two people who are most important to you. What are your responsibilities to them? Why do you find these to be your responsibility? In what ways do you serve them, and how do you feel about the service you provide? This gives you insight into who you are and your purpose. If this person is important to you, then protecting that relationship is part of your purpose.

The single most important person in my life is my wife. She has put up with me and my failings for many years. My responsibility to her is to keep her safe and to help her grow in the ways she wants to grow. I also need to make my ears available to her when she just needs to vent—not solve, just listen. This responsibility is important to me because she is important to me. That is a sufficient reason.

That tells me something about "a" purpose in my life.

What are my most important activities and why?

What things do you do that are most important to you? This also may give you some insight into your purpose. Whether it is the thing you do itself, or what the thing you do allows you to do.

My brother loves playing soccer. Is soccer his purpose? No. However, by playing soccer, he stays physically fit, releases stress, learns teamwork, interacts with friends, makes new friends and a host of other benefits. Those benefits help him towards his actual purpose. If you want to know what that is, you'll have to ask him.

One of the most important things I do is read. This is a way that I learn, it is also a way I escape. I read lots of different types of books, because books will take you anywhere.

When I was in elementary school, my mom went to parent/teacher conferences. My mom was sitting with my math teacher who said I was doing fine and that it was a good thing because 'math is the most important subject.' My mom, who typically kept the peace, said, ' I don't think so. I think it is reading, because if you can read you can teach yourself anything!" My mom started my love of books when I was about 2 years old. Thanks, Mom!

So, I read to get better at listening to people. I read to learn more about how to help people find what they are looking for. I read to find out if Frodo will make it out of Mordor.

For me, my purpose (helping people be confident and efficient) determined the books that I read. This helps me learn how to listen to people and how to help them. The other reading is for my "re-creation," which I need to do daily.

What makes me smile all day?

When I see someone's life change in a positive way, it warms me up inside. When I see a person who was lost and confused one minute, and is now on a track, feeling empowered, feeling like there is hope … wow. I'm not sure what beats that.

What is it in your world that puts a smile on your face that keeps coming back to you as you go through your day? Maybe it's the laugh of a baby, or the smile of a friend. Maybe it is sinking a 30-foot side-hill putt. Perhaps you finally got that picture in your head onto canvas, and it is beautiful! There are as many possibilities here as there are things and ideas. It could be anything.

Understanding why this thing makes you smile will help you to understand a little bit more about what drives you.

Is there something that I feel, if I worked at it, that I could be one of the best in the world?

Do you have one here? For some writers, speakers, and educators, this is where you should spend all your time. Focus on that one skill or ability that you can hone to the finest in the world. Do you have one? Maybe you can be the best photographer in the world, or maybe it's bass guitar, or piano, or soccer, or poetry, or street sweeping or window washing. It doesn't have to be big and glamorous or an "essential activity" (I've hated that term since it got tossed around during the pandemic ... we're *all* essential).

Your purpose is your purpose. If you feel you might be able to be the best in the world, then there is a good chance that your purpose is related to it. Is there a way you can use it to serve others and make a living?

Perhaps writing is mine. Perhaps not! Time will tell.

What comes naturally to me?

Is there something in your life that you've never had to work at, but you're just good at it? This may be a sign that your purpose is in there somewhere. It doesn't mean if you're not naturally good at it that it isn't your purpose. But if there is something like that, there is a good chance that some component of it is part of your purpose.

One thing that has always come naturally to me is 'finding alternatives.' I can look at a problem and find a dozen ways to get to the solution. The bigger trick for me is choosing the 'best' solution and, most importantly, the follow-through. If you're looking for options, I can help you.

How do I best serve people in general?

My definition of service is simply 'doing things for or with others.'

We already talked about serving specific people, but what about society in general? What do you feel is the greatest gift you give to anyone?

For me, I believe it is my desire that everyone feel important and wanted. Essential. Everyone is essential and needs to feel it. I show this by pausing, listening, hugging, and praying with those who need it. I'm better at doing this than I was, but not nearly as good as I will be.

How about you? What do you freely give that helps others?

For what has life prepared me?

We've lived a lot of life. That's a lot of learning opportunities. Sometimes they come to us from out of nowhere.

Back in 1987, I joined Lutheran Youth Encounter (LYE) to travel the world and use music as a way to reach out to people. When I arrived at training in Minneapolis, I met the five people with whom I would be spending the next 14 months. It turned out that all of us were considered decent singers (That's great for harmonizing!). It also turned out that two of us played keyboards and four of us played guitar. Four guitars are too many for a band of six.

One of the LYE staff members told us that someone had donated a bass guitar for our use and wondered if any of us knew how to play. We didn't. But, sensing an opportunity to learn, I volunteered.

The staff member played bass and gave me a half-hour lesson. About six hours later I was on stage playing bass guitar. I say playing ... but was I really playing or was I just standing there making noise with a new instrument? Either way, I had a new job and for the next fourteen months, I played bass. You can learn some things with that much practice. I have now been playing bass for almost forty years and have been playing in my church praise band for the past twenty years or so.

Just a few weeks ago, my friend's band was playing at a restaurant. My wife and I went to listen. I got to relive my "no practice performance" when the bass player took a break and my friend called me up to step in. No rehearsal, no warning. Just like old times. It was a lot of fun and something I never would have been able to do if I hadn't had that unexpected life experience.

No matter how big or how small your experiences are, you are more prepared for life than you were a year ago. Do any of your life events ring out as possibilities for your purpose?

What have you learned through your life that may be of use in your purpose?

What do I want?

This one is so basic I almost forgot to mention it. What do I want? It's a simple thing, but for so many of us, we spend all our time thinking about what is best for the people around us. It's a beautiful idea, but in reality, we serve people best by being the best... 'whatever' ... we were meant to be. And what we want to do tells us a lot. So let yourself think about what you want. Don't worry, no one will know.

Any other questions that you think help you understand yourself a little more?

Ask them here.

Remember, we're just looking for clues here. You have to look at all these answers in the context of the rest of the answers. Perhaps I'm naturally good at shooting free throws (I'm not), but when I run, I fall down a lot (maybe not a lot ...). Perhaps playing basketball is wrong for me, but my purpose may be to teach basketball. Maybe I'm great at talking to kids, and my heart is for reaching out to the poor. Then perhaps my purpose is to start a basketball clinic for challenged inner-city youth.

You can also get some great information from talking to people who know you. I would stick with people who care about you and want to see you succeed. These people will be honest with you and will also be able to give you advice that is consistent with your values.

A stranger may see you as being good with people and offer you a job selling for his gun manufacturing company. A friend might see that you are good with people and also know that you hate guns and want them all banned, so they would suggest you not accept the job.

Some examples of questions you can ask other people:

You've known me for a while, what do you think I'd be good at?

What do my actions tell you about what is important to me?

What do you think I am good at?

I'm still working on finding my place in this world, do you have any thoughts?

Remember, there are no wrong answers here. Just data.

Gather up all of the information and then organize it in whatever way makes sense to you. I think the cloud brainstorm (See Appendix) works well here. Write down all the ideas and see how they fit together. See if there are connections you can make that may not be obvious at first glance.

When you are putting this information down, don't be afraid to add stuff that just comes to mind while you're doing it. Inspiration comes when it wishes.

The odds are with you that this information will give you a very strong direction towards your purpose. Remember to evaluate this considering your values. Your purpose will not be in opposition to your values. If it is, figure out which one you got wrong.

Figuring out which is wrong might take a minute. You really have to dig into them. Ask yourself why it is important to you or why you wrote down that particular value. Look at your answers to those questions. Does anything feel less than "correct"? Maybe one of them needs to be reworded or even abandoned completely.

You may find you have multiple purposes. If that happens, that's okay. You will want to prioritize them. We'll talk more about that in Chapter 4.

Now I want to ask you, "Who do you think you are?" Let's figure it out.

Step-by-Step

Worksheets are available in the appendix or at www.theCoach.vip/SLLOT

5. Ask yourself the questions presented in the chapter and write down the answers.

6. Ask others the questions presented in the chapter and write down the answers.

7. Organize the answers and look for patterns.

Chapter 3
Roles

All the world's a stage, and all the men and women
merely players; They have their exits and their
entrances; and one man in his time plays many parts

— William Shakespeare, *As You Like It*, Act II, Scene 7

What is the most important thing you do?

So far we've talked about your beliefs, values, and principles—who you really are and for what you stand, and purpose—why are you even here? Next up is talking about the roles we play.

Roles are the parts you play. You might be a parent or a boss or a coworker. Really it is any noun that you can fill in the blank for "I am a _____." The noun could be relational (father) or occupational (farmer) or belief (Christian) or anything else. It is part of what makes you unique because no one else has the same combination of roles. See how special you are?

We all have many roles to play. Some last your entire life, some last many years, and some are relatively short. You have more roles than it makes sense to list. What you want to do in this chapter is figure out the most important 5–10 roles that we will work with in the chapter on prioritizing.

The reason we want to look at our roles is not to change what we're doing, but to identify what we do and which of these roles are *most* important. We also want to identify which roles may be self-sabotaging,[7] or imposed by others.

Roles help us in our goal-setting as they give us something to wrap our minds around, something specific we want to improve. One thing to keep in mind when doing this exercise is that these are *your* roles, and the goals you eventually write will apply to *you* in these roles.

For example, in my role as a dad, I can have a goal of being a better communicator with my kids. It wouldn't be appropriate to have a goal to make them listen to me. It will be my goal for me, not my goal for them. We will talk more about this in the chapter on goal setting and the section on life DESIGN.

One role that you have (and so does everyone else) is—you. We all have the role of just being us. We have been working on defining that role as we've been stepping through the book. It underlays the other roles that we play in life.

What other roles do you fill?

There are as many roles as there are people, and actually, more than that. Some examples might be:

- Child
- Spouse
- Parent
- Sibling
- Manager

---

[7] For further discussion on self-sabotage I recommend "The Way out of Self-sabotage; into Self-mastery" by Hunter Charneski

- Christian
- Dog Trainer
- "Fix-it (wo)man"
- Painter
- Friend
- Confidant

Really, it can be anything you do.

It is important to try to identify as many roles as you can and then briefly describe what they mean to you and why.

I am a Christian. It is my most important role. Honestly, I wish I were better at it. This role is important to me because it is my identification of Whose I am and the amazing gift He has given me (eternal life).

As a Christian, there are two key things for which I am responsible.

First: To love God with all my heart, soul, mind, and strength. (Luke 10:27a, paraphrased). This includes worship and prayer and striving to live the life described in the Bible.

Second: to love everyone else as much as I love myself. (Luke 10:27b, paraphrased). This includes such things as being there for other people in times of need or times of celebration, helping others succeed, and most importantly, sharing with them the only way to eternal life.

There is an interesting thing about my role as a Christian. It is a role that I live and it has its own needs, but it is also a strong influence on my other roles. How I operate in my other roles should not violate the 'rules' of my role as Christian. This is in large part because it is my most important role. Do you have a role that does that for you?

The Christian shoemaker does his duty not by putting little crosses on the shoes, but by making good shoes, because God is interested in good craftsmanship.

— *Martin Luther*

Another role I have is that of a husband. As of the writing of this book, my wife has put up with me for nearly 40 years. She is very tolerant.

In my role as husband, it is my job to make sure that my wife feels safe, has what she needs (food, shelter, and daily necessities), that she has opportunities to grow and that she can pursue the purposes of her life.

The Bible says that she should obey me. The Bible also says that I should love my wife and give my life for her.

I believe the role of husband and wife is best summed up in Genesis 2:18 and 2:24 where God says that he will make a helper suitable for him and the two shall become one flesh. The role of the husband is not to boss the wife around—it is to be half of a partnership. Both halves need to be present, active and seeking the best for each other and the relationship.

I have many other roles. Some I'm very good at, some not so much.

Take the time now to look at the roles you have. First just go through and write them down. Then dig into what they mean and why they are important to you.

You have to know what you do before you can determine which is most important to you. Now you're ready to turn the page.

Step-by-Step

Worksheets are available in the appendix or at www.theCoach.vip/SLLOT

8. List as many of your roles as makes sense to you.

9. Write down any thoughts you have about why they are important to you.

Chapter 4
Priorities

"You must do the things you have to do before you can do the things you want to do."

— John Salzwedel

Priority n. the fact or condition of being regarded or treated as more important.

Prioritize v. to list or rate (projects, goals, etc.) in order of priority.[8]

You Can't Do EVERYTHING!

It's an amazing evening. The sun is starting to go down over the trees, but it is still kicking off a little heat. It's about 80 degrees and the IPA in my hand is about 45 degrees, beads of water collect on the side of the bottle.

I'm standing in front of my grill watching the foil packs of potatoes (seasoned perfectly) and the pork chops just starting to sizzle. I prefer the bone-in type. I close the lid of the grill. I've got about 10 minutes before I need to check everything.

My grill is next to my garage, which holds my woodshop. I've got 10 minutes ... and some boards are gently calling to me

---

[8] "prioritize." Merriam-Webster.com. 2025. https://merriam-webster.com/dictionary/prioritize (16 October 2025).

from the shop. So I casually walk that direction. I enter my shop and see the boards, but I tell them that they have to wait because I've been sipping at a beer. Alcohol and table saws do not mix.

I do notice that I had failed to put away some of my other tools during my last project, so I start placing them back in their homes. I get in the groove and am getting a lot done. After about 15 minutes it hits me … burnt food. I move much less casually back to the grill and check on the food. Hmm … Probably okay for me, but I'm not sure Susan will like it. Oops.

Failing to prioritize things in your life can lead to similar, but far more important issues. We set our priorities because there is only so much time in a day, and we can only do one thing at a time. Knowing our priorities helps us be sure that we don't miss the important things because of unimportant things.

Prioritizing helps us to schedule those things that are most important to us (Remember, the things that are most important to the people who are most important to us *are important to us*). We can then fit the stuff of lesser importance into the empty spaces of the day.

Imagine that you have two large jars. You also have some rocks, pebbles, sand, and water.

If you fill one jar with rocks, as many as will fit, you still have room for some pebbles. If you put as many pebbles in as will fit, you will still have room for sand. If you put in as much sand as you can, you still have room for water.

If you fill the other jar with water, you're done. Nothing else will fit without making a mess.

The rocks represent the most important things in your life. You must make room for them. Schedule them *first* so they don't get missed. These may be things like your spouse's birthday, your annual physical checkup, going to church, feeding the dogs, or going to work in the morning.

The pebbles are the things you should get done. Mowing the lawn, washing the dishes, or changing the oil in the car might fall into the "pebble" category. They are important, but not to the core of your being like the "rocks."

The sand represents the things that would be nice to do if you have the time. Organizing the tools in your work area, rearranging the living room, or sorting through your clothes to get rid of stuff you don't like or that doesn't fit are all sand tasks.

The water doesn't really matter if you do it or not. It doesn't really serve a purpose to you, so if you don't do it, you won't care. This could include things like excessive video game playing—you must decide what is excessive. It could be watching police chases on YouTube—this might help you(me) relax, but how much is too much?

Put the rocks into your day first, then the pebbles. Fit the sand and water around the other things. This will add some "flavor" to your day without missing the things you need to get done.

There are 4 main categories that we will be discussing on prioritizing.

People	Tasks
Roles	Ideas

There is a lot of overlap to these. I am a husband (role) to Susan, who hopes that I will not burn the food I'm grilling as the Grillmaster (role) because I am working in my shop as a woodworker (role) Each of these roles were competing for priority in the above story. Let's dissect it.

Husband—my role as husband is to partner with my wife. It is one of my highest priority roles.

Susan—is my wife, and she is the highest priority human being in my life

Grillmaster—grilling in and of itself is not a very high priority for me. I enjoy grilling, but my life would go on just fine if I never grilled again (depressing thought). However, eating food is extremely important. Tasty food is important, but not as important as the food itself.

Woodworker—Putting away a few tools may be important at certain times, but it probably isn't urgent. I can do it later when I have more time and can focus on it.

So, because having tasty food from the grill for my wife and I is a higher priority than putting tools away or cutting a few boards, I now set alarms for myself frequently, so I don't forget what I'm "supposed to be doing."

One key part of dealing with other people is prioritizing. Which relationships are most important to you? We've already looked at our beliefs and values (Chapter 1), so those are our first signposts in decision-making. As these are most important, we strive to NEVER act counter to them. We've looked at the source of our beliefs, and we should stay in sync with what that source tells us to do. Then we look at how our decisions are going to affect those people around us. We want to look at those people in order of their importance to us, and the degree of impact the decision will have on them.

After God and my own values, my highest consideration is for my wife. As long as a decision doesn't go against my beliefs or God's commands, then her needs come first. After my wife comes my kids. As long as a decision doesn't go against God's commands, my beliefs, and my wife's needs, then my kids come next. This is why it is important to figure out your core beliefs and values, so you can apply them when assigning the priority of others in your life.

Prioritizing your roles helps you in deciding how you will spend your time and which goals to go after first. So, in my previous story, my role as grillmaster should take precedence over my role as woodworker. At least at the "food moment." For clarity, this does not mean that I never do woodworker stuff, because grillmaster stuff is more important. It does mean that I should always think about how my actions in one role affect my other roles.

John's role priorities on a beautiful summer evening		John's role priorities on a blizzardy winter evening
Christian (Take care of God's world)	1	**Christian** (Take care of God's world)
Husband (Feeding his bride)	2	**Husband** (Support Susan as needed)
Father (Kids are out of the house)	3	**Father** (Kids are out of the house)
Grillmaster (Cooking a perfect burger)	4	**Woodworker** (Let's build something)
Woodworker (Maybe later)	5	**Grillmaster** (Not tonight)

So, how do we set priorities? Based on our beliefs, values and principles. There is no possible way to write down all the roles/people/things/ideas in your life, so you will just pick out the top ones. Somewhere between five and ten of them. If you want to do more, go ahead, but don't spend the whole day on it. If the roles don't jump out at you rather quickly then they probably aren't that important to you. If you think of one later, then add it. Remember, this is a lifelong process.

Then figure out where each role fits on the priorities scale.

One way might be to assign each one a value of 1-4. Remember, just because something is urgent (or squeaking the loudest) doesn't mean it is important. For tasks it might look like this:

1— **Ultimately important (Rocks).** Must complete these no matter what. And don't be short-sighted—taking care of your physical health is ultimately important.

2— **Important (Pebbles).** This is important and I should do this if it won't prevent me from completing a category "1."

3— **Somewhat Important (Sand).** If I have some spare time and get around to it, these things are relevant.

4— **Unimportant (Water).** It doesn't matter if I ever do it, but it can add some variety to my day when I've got space for it.

This is useful in scheduling the limited time and energy you have available.

Priority—Work

A woman has been out of work for 6 months. The family has been having trouble getting by. She and her husband really need to make more money than he currently does on his own. They are currently 3 months behind on their mortgage, and some other bill collectors are starting to call.

She is trained in marketing and has been trying hard to find a job in her field.

One day she is offered a job making a decent wage. It's driving a school bus. She used to do that but quit because she just didn't enjoy it.

Should she take it? There are a lot of people these days who would say 'no, she shouldn't take it because she doesn't like doing that.' But those people are missing something. *We don't know what her priorities are.*

If her highest priority is having a job (Role: Worker) she can enjoy, and she will happily live in a small apartment to allow that, then perhaps she should say "no."

Perhaps they have several kids (Role: Mom), and they are already in as small a place as they believe they could comfortably live. In this case, maybe she should take the job if her kids are her higher priority.

Perhaps her role as a partner with her husband (Role: Wife) is her most important role and she feels that it is unfair to not be working outside the home when he is.

You see, we don't know what her priorities are, and we should never judge someone even if we do.

This is why we examine ours now, so that when decisions come up, we can easily see what is important to us, and this helps us to move in alignment with our beliefs.

Where you're going to work and what work you're going to do is a huge decision and for most, a high priority. It needs to be consistent with your values and something that will make enough money to cover your needs. If you are an animal rights activist, then being a trapper may not be the right choice for you because it violates your values. Inconsistencies here will create stress in your life.

There are times in our lives when we need to take jobs that maybe aren't ideal for us, but we need to make money to pay the bills or to support the people who are important to us. In these situations, we still need to be consistent with our values, but we may not need to enjoy the job at this moment. We should still give our best and do a good job. After all, someone is giving us their money in order to do a task for them.

As I write this book, I have an internal conflict. Nothing big, but it is there. The conflict is this: Do I write another chapter or do I finally organize part of my woodshop so I can find a tape measure when I need it?

Writing this book hits a number of my priorities. I truly believe this information can help people live a better life. That's important to me. I feel that completing this book will be a big achievement and will provide me with a sense of accomplishment. That is important to me. There are others, but those two are pretty high up on my list.

Right now, the mess in my shop isn't really delaying anything for me or others. It is a little frustrating for me sometimes, but only because it violates my sense of order. No one is being inconvenienced or hurt. Just slightly annoyed.

Consequently, the book comes first. Hopefully I will have organized my shop by the time you read this, but things happen, and until it is a higher priority for me than other things, it won't be done.

If my wife desperately needed me to make something in my shop, and I couldn't find the tools I needed to make it, then her need would move "cleaning the mess" up higher in my priority list. That's how life and prioritizing work. It is fluid, so you need to know what's important to you.

Think about a situation in your life right now where you are feeling a bit unsettled. Compare your actions with the priorities and roles you've already figured out. Is there a conflict? Is something out of order?

Take some time to figure out who and what is most important to you. Don't be afraid to find a professional to teach or guide you. Once you've done that, it will be time to figure out what you're going to do with/for them!

Step-by-Step

Worksheets are available in the appendix or at www.theCoach.vip/SLLOT

10. Identify the 10 roles that are most important to you and why. Get a general idea of their priority for you. Number them if you can. Put them in that order.

Chapter 5
Success and Goals

Everybody wants to rule the world.

— Tears for Fears

True happiness is not contained in what you get.
Happiness is contained in what you become.

— Jim Rohn

What is success? We hear lots of ideas from lots of people. It seems to usually revolve around money, or houses, or cars. Maybe a nice watch. But are those things really important to you? Maybe a little bit, but not a lot? Maybe a lot? Maybe it's climbing Mount Everest, or running a super-marathon, or swimming across Lake Michigan.

TV will tell you that success is wealth and power. Social media makes it pretty clear that success is lots of 'likes', fancy dining, and being the most popular. There is nothing wrong with these goals. But are they yours? Are they really yours? Or are they yours because it looks like all those things make those online people happy—and you want to be happy too?

We hear discussions about successful people, and we envy them. It seems easy to identify successful people. They have shiny new cars, big houses, and a great job title. People write stories about them and interview them for their TV shows. They've got it all.

That begs the question; "Why do so many of these people end up depressed or even suicidal?"

Looks can be deceiving, and social media is great at promoting deception. We see the outward 'shiny' but not the darkness on the inside. People don't post about their everyday, mundane lives.

Everyone only posts their greatest hits. No B-sides.[9]

— Jimmy Palmer, *NCIS*, Season 14, Episode 13

So, perhaps they aren't really successful. They have all the outward trappings of success without the actual success. Perhaps they are not happy because they are too focused on "stuff." Success doesn't need to have anything to do with stuff. Success can be people, or experiences, or feelings. The darkness inside comes from going after the wrong things for the wrong reasons.

We spend more time planning our weekends than our lives. If these "outwardly successful people" are truly happy—that is awesome. Even if they are it is unlikely that the exact same things that make them happy will make you happy. So don't use their benchmark.

What is success? To me it is the attainment of those "things" which are important to me.

---

[9] If you are unfamiliar with the term "B-side", it comes from the days of 45 RPM recording singles. The "A-side" would be an expected hit. You could turn the record over and play the "B-side" which was another song, but one not expected to be a hit, though sometimes it was.

For you, it is the attainment of those things which are important to *you*.

It doesn't matter if I think your definition of success is good enough. It has to come from you, or it won't provide you with any energy or fulfillment.

Design your own HAPPY. Figure out what will make you happy. Use that to help define your success. This may change as you age, but it won't be the "flavor of the week." It's a deeper 'happy' than a quick feel-good hit. **Happiness is contentment**. A feeling or the knowledge that "this feels right and is good."

But what does success mean to *you*? It is important to define our success for several reasons. When we define success for ourselves:

1. We know what we're aiming for

2. We don't feel like slackers if our success doesn't include some grandiose event

3. We don't get sidetracked by things that don't really matter to us

Figuring out what success looks like to you and combining that with your Beliefs and Values (Chapter 1) are the keys to not leaving life on the table. When you have these items aligned and your actions are congruent, you will achieve success. We tend to get those things we focus on, so, we need to figure out on what we wish to focus.

Content vs Complacent (An Aside for Christians)

Are you seeking to be content or complacent? Is it against the teachings of the Bible to have ambition? Is it wrong? I'm not a theologian, but I have thought about this question a lot. I have always sought to improve myself, and at times it seemed to me that my dissatisfaction with where I was conflicted with Paul's teachings in the Bible.

> *I have learned, in whatever situation I am,*
> *to be content.*
>
> — Philippians 4:11b ESV

If I am supposed to be content, then the status quo should be fine, but it never has been.

Here's what I have been able to figure out on this: I believe that we should seek constant improvement in ourselves. We should consistently work on our skills, our relationships with God, others, and ourselves. The key is to know that our own worth is not derived from those successes and failures, nor does our security depend on them. Our worth comes from the fact that we were individually created by God, and our security comes from our being valued by Him and His promises to care for us. We can be content and happy in that knowledge. But that does not mean we sit around and just accept the life that shows up. We were created with a mind and a will. We can learn how to improve our lives and the lives of others.

You exist for a purpose. Use the skills you have in order to achieve that purpose.

Now, I know some of you reading this may not be believers, but the importance of the distinction still exists. Based on dictionary definitions, happiness is a positive feeling that can be either short- or long-term. Complacency is just accepting that everything is the way it is and there is nothing we can do about it, so we won't try. Contentment is a long, drawn-out, peaceful happiness. It is accepting the current state, and that we have innate value as we are. Contentment also believes that we can make life even better, but remains at peace either way.

So, we seek contentment. We seek improvement in our world and our lives while being content with who we are.

It is a subtle distinction, but it makes all the difference.

Goals

In Section III of this book, called DESIGN, we talk about dreaming (Chapter 10). We talk about finding what that "perfect life" looks like for you. That thing or those things which ultimately are what you are seeking for your life. Goals are the same concept but sometimes they might be a little shorter and a little smaller in scale. They also make up the small steps in your life DESIGN (Chapter 14).

Perhaps your overall dream is to be a marathon runner and to have 3% body fat. Perhaps your intermediate goals are to run a half marathon and to have 15% body fat then 10% then 8% then 6%. We move step-by-step to the intermediate goals.

A well-designed goal will give you energy, it will help you to see the steps that you need to take. If you dream clearly enough and describe your goals clearly enough and most importantly, describe "why" you want that goal, then you will have energy every day to go after those goals. If you want to lose 20 pounds so your favorite hat fits better, that may be a good driver for you. It may not. Perhaps you want to lose 20 pounds so that you can walk up the stairs without your knees aching the entire way. Maybe you want to lose 20 pounds so you can play with your kids longer. If the "why" of your goal is important enough to you, you will always be able to figure out the how. It won't always be quick or easy, but if it is important enough, you'll find a way.

What is a goal?

Walt Disney said that 'a dream is a wish your heart makes.' Well, I think a goal is a wish your mind makes, with the full approval of your heart. A goal is a specific element of the "you" you are trying to be.

I don't think we set enough goals as a society. We have a lot of "wouldn't it be nice-es" but no structure behind them. Perhaps that is because a lot of people just don't know how to move forward. No one has ever shown them how to go from idea to reality. Or perhaps it is true that some people are just happy complaining about the way things ought to be. You're reading this book, so that probably isn't you.

You have most likely heard that your goals should be SMART goals.

- Specific
- Measurable
- Attainable
- Relevant
- Time-Bound

We're not going to spend much time on this, as an internet search will give you all the info you need. Many very bright people have written on it at length.

In general, I believe that in a setting where a group of people need to be on the same page, SMART goals are awesome. Everyone has the same playbook and the same measurements.

And, if SMART goals work for you personally—then keep using that methodology.

That being said, I think we need a new way to look at personal goals. Our personal goals may not be easily quantified:

"I want to improve the way I communicate with my children."

Measurable doesn't really work.

Attainable. I don't like this restriction on a goal at all.

The four-minute mile is impossible. According to doctors, your heart would explode. Then in 1954 Roger Bannister broke the four-minute mile. Since then, it has been broken over 2000 times. In fact, in early 2025 a 15-year-old from New Zealand (Sam Ruthe) ran the mile in 3 minutes and 58 seconds.

Everything is attainable. The only question is whether you are willing to do what it takes to achieve it. As I've said many times—"there is always a solution."

Time-bound is important, but I think at a personal level, for *some* things, time limits put undue pressure on us and can be negative for our mental health and our success. I believe if we set a goal and start *now*, we're good.

If you set a goal to lose 50 pounds in 6 months (very doable), but you only lose 40—the underlying message is that you failed, when actually losing 40 pounds is a great success and you should be proud of what you've accomplished. In personal goals, we need to be more focused on moving in the right direction. And, if we're being honest, that's how businesses look at goals all the time. "Yes, we had a goal of a 10% increase in revenue this year. We only had 7% and we're so proud of our team achieving that in these trying times." I can't tell you how many times I've heard something similar in a company meeting.

So, let's look at goal setting in a different way. Let me introduce you to **D-MAC**. D-MAC is a goal-setting paradigm that fits everyday life.

- "D" is for describable.

  This allows us to have a goal on things that cannot be quantified or measured, or that don't have a specific end line. "I want to eat better and exercise more so that I can think a little clearer and feel less stressed." These end results are completely subjective and yet still tell us what we are seeking to do and why. The purpose here is to describe what you are after in a way that leaves no doubt what you are trying to do. This is a description that can be read by anyone, and they will know what you mean.

- "M" is for motivating.

  The goal has to fire you up. Give you energy. Give a reason to get out of bed in the morning and the energy to create a new habit. You need to be able to understand and explain **why** this goal is important to you. If you don't know why or if the why isn't important to you, it will slip away from you and two months from the day you set the goal, you will be in the same place you started.

New habits aren't easy, they take work. If the goal isn't something you really want, then it is unlikely you will have the energy and focus to do what it takes to achieve that goal. The same is true if it is a goal that someone gives you. There is no energy there. One thing I learned in my many years in management and leadership is that if you want to demotivate someone—give them a goal they don't believe in.

- "A" is for aligned.

Your goal has to be in line with your own values. If it isn't, you will sabotage yourself

> *When in doubt, check if your actions are*
> *aligned with your purpose.*

— Azim Jamal & Brian Tracy, *What You Seek Is Seeking You*

- If you value nature, then you might not want a goal of paving your property for a private tennis court.
- If you don't value animals as pets, you may not want to open a dog obedience school.

- "C" is for chunk-able.

Chunking is the process of dividing a large task into smaller, more manageable tasks.

> *Nothing is particularly hard*
> *if you divide it into small jobs.*
>
> — *Henry Ford*

The only hard part about chunking is knowing how small we need to break the tasks.

The answer? Make them as small as you can to make sure you achieve successes.

So, when you make your goals, either now, or later in this book, or on New Years Eve, make sure you describe them so well that you can taste them or feel how good achieving them will feel. Make sure that the goal really turns you on and that you understand why. Make sure that the goal does not violate any of your values. Then be sure that you can break the goal achievement into steps, and that you write down the very first step you are going to take.

You can have lots of goals, but don't work on too many at once or you will find yourself not accomplishing any of them.

The man who chases two rabbits
will catch neither of them.

— Confucius

Keep in mind, sometimes as you go through the steps, you will need to adjust the next step. That is because the more you learn, and the closer you get to your goal, the clearer you will see it. We'll talk through all of these concepts a bit more in Section III-DESIGN.

Step-by-Step

Worksheets are available in the appendix or at www.theCoach.vip/SLLOT

11. Describe what success looks like to you.

Section II
Others in Your Life

How you are remembered after you are gone is only
important in that it shows others their importance
to you and the lessons you've taught.

—John Salzwedel

Your life is like a play with several acts. Some of the
characters who enter have short roles to play, others
much larger. Some are villains and others are good
guys. But all of them are necessary; otherwise, they
wouldn't be in the play.

—Wayne Dyer

To **Stop Leaving Life on the Table,** you have to get your relationships right. How we interact with others will in large part determine our success. We can't do it alone. There are no true self-made successes. Everyone has had help somewhere. Others help us; we help them. This is how we all have success.

Your beliefs and values will have a large impact on not only who you interact with, but also how. The better you understand *you* and what is important to you, the better you can understand how you and others can work together in life.

How you treat others determines how others see you.

I was having lunch with a business associate one day. It was a nice restaurant, not fancy. It was the busy lunch time rush. Our server was working hard to take care of everyone, and honestly doing a very good job.

She came to our table and it became very clear that to my associate she was not as important as he was. He was matter-of-fact, 'take my order and go away. Don't come back until you have my food, unless I need something else which you'd better anticipate.' I was truly embarrassed.

I understand that we were there to eat. She was there to work. But the total lack of courtesy and recognition that she was a human being with as many hopes and dreams as he had, maybe more, was shocking to me. I lost a lot of respect for that man that day. It certainly wasn't the kind of impression that increased the amount of money I spent with his company.

Treat people like people. They deserve it.

The most memorable people in your life will be the
ones who loved you when you were not very lovable.
Remember this and return the favor.

— H Jackson Brown Jr.

Relationships are Key

All success depends on relationships. Relationships help us understand ourselves and others better. There are three broad categories of our relationships: with God (/spirit/universe/ divine, whatever you identify with), with others, and with ourselves. All of your relationships fall into one of these categories.

Not Leaving your Life on the Table is dependent on these relationships. In fact, your definition of success is created by these relationships and their importance to you.

In this section, we will be talking about these three categories of relationships and why they are so important. We will discuss different types of relationships and what may fall within them. You need to determine where they fall in your list of priorities, as they are different for each of us.

Before we get into individual groups, let's talk about some needs that are common to nearly everyone.

Needs Common to Everyone

We all have needs, and there are many that are common to most people.

Acceptance

The first one I want to mention is Acceptance. People need to know that you accept them as they are. It doesn't mean that you approve of everything they do, but that no matter what they do, you recognize their inherent value.

They are important just because they are. They have value just because they are. Can they be better? Of course! None of us are perfect and we should be constantly trying to improve *ourselves*. But we can't improve anyone else. Only they can do that. We can and should be there to support them as they try to improve themselves and try to make changes, but we can't change them.

Keep in mind, whoever the other person is, they are just as good and just as valuable as you are. Perhaps you do more good things than they do, but that doesn't make you better or worth more. It just means you're further down the road in your decision-making ability or that you have been blessed with more opportunities. Accept people as they are. Walk alongside them as they try to grow—and as you grow. When you walk alongside someone, they are walking alongside you. Win-win.

Support and Encouragement

When we want to accomplish something, it is so much easier when we know someone is in our corner. Any time we are trying something new or learning different ideas, it is a struggle. It is hard work. If we have someone telling us, 'You can do it,' it is far more likely that we will succeed.

One of the worst things we can do to someone who is trying to grow is to laugh at them when they fail or tell them to just give up when it is hard.

Be the one that helps them believe in themselves.

Safety and Security

We all want to feel safe and secure in our home. We want to know that we can relax and feel some degree of comfort in that home. We want it to be clean (You define what clean means to you.), and open, a refuge from the world outside. How we choose to create that situation is entirely up to us and takes into account our needs and our means as well as the needs of those around us.

Being Heard

Have you ever been trying to talk to a group and had them just keep talking over you? I sure have. There is one particular group that I am a part of that makes me think that either 1) my voice is too soft or 2) the others are losing their hearing or 3) they just don't believe I have anything important to say. Because I know and trust and care about all these people, I give them the benefit of the doubt and believe it is a combination of numbers 1 and 2 above.

But what if I wasn't as self-confident, or I didn't know them ... I may lean into number 3. And that hurts. We all like to feel valued and one great way to show someone they are important to us is to listen. Hear them. Ask them clarifying questions.

I'm not talking about that listening that ends with: "... uh huh, so," and then an abrupt subject change. That is dismissive and annoying. When we half-listen and then change the subject, we communicate to others around us that we don't really care what they have to say.

Presence

Being there.

When I need someone to talk to, I need someone to talk to. I'll be honest, there are days when I feel like no one is there for me, except God, and I even doubt Him sometimes. Now, I know it isn't true—but it is hard to feel accepted or listened to when you can't find anyone to talk to. We are all very busy (too busy?) and we cannot always be there for everyone. There simply isn't enough time in the day. But everyone needs this— so it is important that we have our priorities straight.

It is also important that we listen so we may hear those times when people are in need. I guarantee, no matter how much you work on it, you will miss opportunities to be there for someone. You may reach out to them a little too late, so forgive yourself and then reach out anyway. Knowing that someone cares for you a day late is much better than never hearing it.

Observing how you treat people you disagree with
is the most robust way to understand what you've
learned about kindness, love and compassion.

— Unknown

We're now going to lean into those specific relationships and some needs that may be specific to them. The list isn't exhaustive; use your listening skills to find the ones that aren't discussed here. They are your relationships ... understanding them is *your* responsibility.

Are there any people in your life that you have trouble dealing with? If you said no, then, in the words of a pastor friend of mine, 'the truth is not in you.'

We all have people in our lives that cause us stress. Hopefully we each have even more people that help us deal with stress. Have you noticed that the people who help us deal with stress are sometimes the same people who cause us stress? Do you reach out and help people who are in stressful situations? Do you also cause at least some stressful situations? I know I do!

When I sold my company, part of the deal was that I would work for the new company for a while.

Do you think I both felt and caused stress there? I was a former CEO who had been running the same type of company for many years, and I was trying to fit into a company that did nearly everything differently. My suggestions weren't always well received, and that was not well received by me. We had different ways of doing things. I knew my way was the right way and my new bosses knew their way was better. Guess what? I was in their company now. Whether I agreed or not, I had to do things their way. That is not a well-developed skill for me. It was very stressful for them and for me.

Some of the stress came from pride, there's no doubt about that. But it also came from my perception of needs not being met. In this short description above (which is much less complicated than real life), my perception was that my needs for "being heard", "acceptance", and "support and encouragement" were not being met. This created a tense environment for me. That tension created a bad situation for them too.

Working with others is part of life, and we need to do our best to understand them. In Chapter 4 when we talked about priorities, one of the first things I mentioned was our relationship with God. We're going to dig into that a little more here.

How well are you and God getting along?

Chapter 6

God

*When God contemplates some great work, He
begins it by the hand of some poor, weak, human
creature, to whom He afterwards gives aid.*

— Martin Luther

If you do not believe in a creator God, this chapter still has
thoughts for you. I would suggest you read this chapter from
the viewpoint of whatever controls your worldview. It may be
money or politics or science or people or something entirely
different. Sometimes it will be easy to make the mental switch
on point-of-view. Sometimes it will be nearly impossible. Take
the time to really think about the concepts and how you may be
able to use them, don't just dismiss them "out of hand." For you,
the chapters on relationships to others and yourself are going
to be a bigger driver toward designing your life. Do your best.

A man was tired. He had been walking for days. He was
beaten up, both physically and mentally. He felt the pangs
of hunger and thirst. 'I can't go on, I have nothing left. I am
ready to be done.' He sat down under a tree and fell asleep.

He was startled awake and found that someone had left food
for him. Though still exhausted, he heard in his mind that if

he had any hope of going on, he had to eat. So he ate. The food did little to assuage his hunger, but it tasted good. It was nice to have something in his stomach. He wondered aloud who left the food. Was there really someone who cared for him?

Still tired and with a full belly … he quickly fell back asleep, but was again awoken. There was more food. He found he was again hungry, so he ate again. And felt refreshed.

He continued his long journey on foot. Step-by-step-by-step. He walked through forests and deserts, across streams and valleys and found himself standing on the side of a mountain, where he waited to hear the voice of God.

It came in a gentle whisper.

(*paraphrase of* 1 Kings 19:3–12 *by the author*)

Our Relationship to God

Getting the most out of your life starts with your relationship to God. More than any other chapter, this one will have some biases. I am a Christian and my viewpoint on this is decidedly and unapologetically Christian. I believe that having a relationship with the God that created each of us is important.

For those of us who do believe in a God who created everything, including us, we have to build that relationship with Him.

In developing our relationship with God, we must get to know Him. What is His nature? How does He want us to be? How does He interact with us? What do we really know about Him? As with anyone, or anything, we get to know Him by talking, listening, reading and sharing. God wants to be in a relationship with us. He gave us prophets, thousands of years ago, as well as His written word. Today we have that written word available to us. We can examine it ourselves. We also have other people who can help us in getting to know God.

There have been hundreds, even thousands of books written on the topic of knowing God. In this chapter we will discuss several ways that I have used to get to know, and to communicate with God. These are not presented in any particular order, nor are the descriptions exhaustive. There are lots of experts on these areas who can teach you the details on how these work.

Prayer

Prayer is having a conversation with God. It is an open dialog. It can contain praise, worship, thanksgiving, confession, requests, intercession, singing, and silence. This is a time when we tell God how important He is to us, we acknowledge His divinity and His "awesomeness." It is a time when we can tell Him what is bothering us and ask for His advice. We can sing songs and enjoy His presence. We can sit quietly and listen for His "still small voice" (1 Kings 19:12b KJV).

There is no shortage of books on prayer. One of my favorites is *The Hour that Changes the World* by Dick Eastman.

Bible Study

Bible Study is an intensive reading of the Bible. It can be done either by focusing on one book, or on a specific topic. It is reading the Bible, comparing translations, studying the writings of theologians on the topic. It is a deep, intensive dive into what the Bible actually says and what that means to you in your life, every day.

Devotions

Devotions tend to be topical and are often guided by a devotional book. Typically, a time of devotions opens with prayer and a bible reading. Then the devotional is read. It may be a story or a thought. It can be anything that gets us focused on the topic at hand and God's role in that topic. After contemplating the devotional, we close in prayer.

Meditation

Meditation is focused listening. It will often begin with reading a Bible verse. That verse will then serve as the focal point of our minds. We think about the verse and listen for God to provide us understanding and insight on what it means.

Reading/Listening

Reading is reading! Find a book about God and read it.

The risk here is that *anyone* can write a book. It doesn't have to be true or accurate. Find out about the author. Ask trusted friends for recommendations. Look for reading lists from people who are known to be faithful to what you believe. Most importantly, check the information against scripture. If the author "corrects" something in scripture or interprets scripture in a way that seems "weird," then check with your spiritual leader before reading on.

Listening is taking the time to hear a speaker or listen to a recording. It's a lot like reading, just a different format. The same rules apply for being cautious.

Worship

When we hear worship, we typically think of gathering at a place, singing some songs, hearing someone speak and praying. This can absolutely be worship. I have been a part of the same congregation in West Michigan for many decades. On Sunday morning, you can usually find me there attending a worship service and hanging out with my friends.

But worship doesn't have to be anywhere in particular. It is anytime, anywhere. It is being in the presence of God and letting Him know that you think He's pretty cool.

Fellowship

Life can be hard. It is even harder on your own. Fellowship is a time when we get together with others who believe as we do. We share knowledge, support each other. Help each other. It can take place at a worship service, at a Bible Study, a church picnic, golf league, a retreat, even a "church clean-up day." It is anytime that you gather with other believers in a spirit of caring and support.

I've often heard people say that they spend time getting to know God in nature, they don't need to fellowship with others. It's great to get to know God in nature. He is there; we can get to know Him better there. But in our society, we absolutely need others to lean on. There are too many things pulling us away from God.

Works of Service

We get to know God a little bit during works of service. When we are helping others who are in need, we get a tiny little glimpse of the world through God's eyes. We see people as important. We see people in their weakest. We help people without judging them.

It is a time we act like the people we wish we were all the time.

Giving

There are three types of giving that I hear explained: Time, Talents and Treasures. We talk about all of them in this book.

We give to those things which are most important to us. We can use our time, talents and treasures in the service of God and His church.

We talk about prioritizing in another chapter. When we spend our resources, we learn more about what is important to us.

We also give in gratitude to God. He has given us everything. We give back to the church and to others in need in gratitude for that. He doesn't need us, or our time, or our talents. He can accomplish His goals without us. He *wants* us to be a part of it because that brings us closer to Him.

Fasting

According to scriptures, fasting is giving up food for a period of time. Other forms of fasting exist, such as fasting from social media, alcohol, or even speaking. The purpose is to focus on God and His provisions for you. It is also to humble yourself before God and to open yourself up to His teaching and guidance. It is done to earnestly seek God in prayer. So, beyond just not eating, fasting includes prayer and meditation.

Being Quiet

> *"Be still, and know that I am God."*
>
> — Psalm 46:10 ESV

Take the time to sit quietly and enjoy God's presence and listen for his words.

Have you ever talked to God? Have you ever heard Him? It's strange and humbling when it happens. I've been blessed to experience it more than once.

Sometimes it is like actual words in your head, and sometimes it is more of an impression on your heart.

Whichever way, you'll know it when it happens.

The voice of God will never contradict scripture, so keep that in mind.

Knowing God goes far beyond head knowledge. We can learn all the facts by sticking our nose in a book and never coming up for air, but until we stop and listen, and spend the time feeling and hearing, we won't truly know God.

Take the time to develop your relationship with God. It takes work. It takes time. It takes effort. If you believe you were created by God, then getting to know Him will help you to understand yourself better.

Step-by-Step

Worksheets are available in the appendix or at www.theCoach.vip/SLLOT

12. Who is your God or your driving force?

13. What are some ways you can get to know God or your truth better?

Chapter 7

Spouse

*A happy marriage is the union of
two good forgivers.*

— Ruth Bell Graham

This chapter is on your relationship with your spouse. This can include a "significant other," but there are some limits there. There is a difference between a spouse and a significant other. The commitment isn't the same. The responsibility isn't the same.

No matter what your marital status is (decidedly single, currently single, engaged, long-term committed relationship …) there is information here on how to interact with others. Read the information and consider how it applies to you and yours.

As I have already said, the most important human relationship to me is the one with my wife. These are my "glasses" here.

We made vows to each other way back in 1989. Those promises are no less valid today than they were back then.

I promised before God and a whole church full of witnesses that I would love her, care for her, partner with her through good and bad, and that I would put her first before all people.

I've not been perfect. But I keep trying.

Here are the most important needs I see in this relationship. There are more, and every relationship is different. But I think you will find these needs appear for nearly every couple. I have repeated the "common to all" here with some examples that are specific to spouses.

Need to Be Heard

The first and most important of your spouse needs (and it is true for all relationships) is the need to be heard. And that doesn't just mean to hear the words. It means to listen for the meaning. As Stephen Covey puts it, "Listen to understand."

We tend to be so insecure in our own beliefs that our listening is done with the purpose of responding instead of just listening to the other person. (That's another reason to nail down your beliefs first, so you don't need to figure out what you believe when you should be listening)

You married your spouse for a reason. Hopefully it was because you felt you would be better as a team than as two individuals.

If you are operating as a team, then you both provide part of the equation. You know finance, your spouse knows car repair. You're both pretty good at cooking, so you take turns.

Have you ever seen a football team where one player thinks he has to do all the jobs? You will never see that team win a championship

Get feedback. This is true on projects, but it is also true on life. "How can I help your day to be better?" "Is there anything I do that is causing extra work for you?"

Then listen to the answer and do something about it. It really doesn't matter if you agree. If the other person perceives it to be true, then talk through and find a solution that works.

It isn't really that hard to know what you should do.

The steps for listening are:

1) Make eye contact (if possible)
2) Turn off or put down the TV/Radio/Computer/Book/ Newspaper/Magazine
3) Be quiet
4) Ask clarifying questions (not argumentative questions)
5) When the person is done explaining, repeat back to them what you understand to see if you heard it right
6) Repeat steps 3-5 until you have it right

You will be amazed at the power of this one simple skill.

Need to Be Accepted

We all have the need to be accepted. Just as we are. Accept your spouse as he or she is. They have inherent value. It is important that they know that you value them and believe in them.

It doesn't mean you will or should approve of everything they do. There are, and should be consequences for actions, and sometimes that can be painful. Even if it comes to a point when you can no longer live with that person, it is important that they know that they are still worth something.

You may not be able to accept their actions, but they are not their actions. It is important that we acknowledge their value. This can really be hard to do when someone has wronged you.

Need to Feel Secure

We all have the need for security.

Food, water, and shelter are very basic. Sixty years ago in the U.S. the job as primary breadwinner went to the husband, while the wife took care of acquiring the food, cleaning the house and raising the kids. It isn't necessarily that way anymore. That set up still exists. But now, the exact opposite exists as well. And even more common is the dual income, everyone-chip-in-where-needed family dynamic.

We all need food, shelter, and clothing.

Spouses now work together to provide that. You as an individual need to be doing your part in providing these things with your spouse or significant other.

Many years ago, I tried my hand selling real estate. I was pretty good at handling the details of a transaction. I was not very good at creating enough transactions. I was working full-time trying to make money.

My wife was also working full-time and actually making money. She did most of the cooking and cleaning, too. I did the maintenance, ate the food, and tried to build the business.

For that particular part of our life, she was providing the food and shelter. When kids came along, it needed to change somehow. We decided, as a team, that I would take a 9-5 job so she could work part-time and be home with the kids. Going forward I would be providing the food and shelter.

The dynamics are always changing, but it is your responsibility to make sure your spouse has his/her basic living needs met. It might mean taking a job you don't like in order to pay the bills. It might mean reshuffling your house-hold roles in order to allow the other spouse to work. It is your responsibility to make sure it happens.

Safety

There's something that should go without saying—but I'm going to say it anyway.

Your spouse has the need (and the right) to feel safe in their own home.

Sometimes our financial situation may cause us to live in an area that maybe isn't all that safe. We should be making sure doors have locks, windows have latches. Maybe a dog, maybe an alarm system, cameras, whatever.

We should also be sure we're not encouraging unsafe situations. Don't hang around with violent people, don't have your property be conducive to illegal activity (Have good lighting etc.) and keep the home in good repair.

At the top of the list—your spouse should never be afraid of you. If he/she is, then get help. If you are violent when you drink—stop drinking. If you can't watch a football game without screaming and throwing things, then don't watch football. At least not with your spouse.

Your spouse should never expect anything but love to come from your hand.

If you don't feel safe in your own home, then reach out for help. Don't just accept it.

Forgiveness

Your spouse is going to disappoint you at some point. They will forget your birthday or your anniversary. They will throw away something you wanted to keep. They will spend money on something that isn't important to you. It will happen.

You will do it too.

Forgive them.

Holding grudges will kill a relationship. It will also kill you inside. Reliving the insult will take your joy and energy away. It will also make your spouse feel like something less than the person you once put on a pedestal.

Don't do that.

Recreation

PLAY! It's fun. Your spouse wants to have fun with you. You want to have fun with your spouse.

Recreation (RE-CREATION) is necessary to get our energy back, to release tension. Laughter keeps you and your marriage healthy.

Enjoy each other's company. Enjoy being together.

Have sex. Remind your spouse of your playfulness on your wedding night. He/she needs to know that you still find him/her attractive. Sex in marriage is not something you should be ashamed of. It is good for you mentally, physically, emotionally and spiritually. Enjoy it guilt-free!

Your spouse should be the most important person in your life. Treat them like it. Take care of them. Lift them up. Listen to them. Love them. Appreciate them.

You'll both feel better for it. You will both feel more appreciated, heard and loved. Having fun together fills many of our basic needs and many of our wants.

Step-by-Step

Worksheets are available in the appendix or at www.theCoach.vip/SLLOT

14. What are some things you can do, that you are not already doing, to improve your relationship with your spouse? Write them down.

15. Ask your spouse to tell you about their goals and dreams. Use your new listening skills.

Chapter 8

Other Family Members

There is a crazy person in every family.
If there isn't one in yours, then it is probably you.

As you design your life and go after your goals, your days will intermingle with many family members and friends. How and where we interact with them can affect our direction, our moods, our focus and ultimately whether or not we Leave Life on the Table. It is important that we acknowledge some of the challenges and opportunities that may arise out of these relationships.

How varied can we get in our discussion of relationships with family members? You will find every kind of relationship in your family. Healthy ones, horrible ones, supportive, destructive, enlightening, jaw-dropping, head-shaking, and blood-pressure-raising.

There is no way to go through all the different family relationships that exist. Yours may differ from these completely, but here are a few. The basic idea is to understand that you have many types of relationships in your family and the needs within them are pretty consistent.

Children

Kids are the greatest joy you will ever have and the hardest work you will ever do. You will try your best and fail (there is no owner's manual). They will forgive you for your failings or they won't. They will make you prouder than you ever thought possible, and then they will make decisions that make you shake your head. They will not accept your advice, and they will learn from you. They are quickest at learning our bad habits, so watch your choices.

One of the things that I think we as parents forget most often is that children have the same need to be heard that we have. They don't have as much information as we have (they haven't been around for as long), but they sometimes have more information than we think they do (we aren't with them 24/7 or in their heads). Just like relating to our spouses, we need to listen. Don't assume they are wrong, and you are right. They are far more likely to listen to you if you listen to them first.

Keep in mind that you know the things you do because you made mistakes. You didn't listen all the time growing up. Let them make mistakes. Prevent the ones that will hurt them if you can, but the ones that won't hurt them—let them go. If they want to shave their head, let them. It'll grow back.

I've heard it said there are two rules to keep in mind.

1) Don't sweat the small stuff
2) It's all small stuff

This is wrong, especially when raising kids. It isn't all small stuff. There are times when you need to sweat. You need to have difficult conversations. You need to explain some very embarrassing things. According to the National Institute of Health, a human's decision-making capability does not fully develop until around age 25.

Children need our help to avoid serious issues. But not by command, by discussion. Talk to them about it. When you have a history of listening and hearing, you can have a great conversation with your children on important topics.

When your children reach adulthood, they will still need your help, but they will also want to prove to you that you raised them well and they can make it on their own. Be slow to jump in and fix things. Wait for them to ask for your help.

Call them or stop in to see them. In most cases they want to see you.

Parents

If you are reading this book and you are still living in your parents' home, I want to remind you of a couple of things.

1) It is their house, their rules. They do have the right to tell you what to do. Hopefully they will have read the paragraph above and you can sit down and have a good conversation and come to an understanding. No guarantees.

2) Your parents didn't get an owner's manual when you were born. You are a complex machine and learning microcomputer all in one bundle. Figuring out how you think, and feel is so very hard. They will get it wrong sometimes. Cut them some slack and try to have a conversation about it. Don't argue with them (see rule #1). But hopefully they are reasonable and

when you say, "I will do what you say, and could you please help me understand your rationale because I don't." Use <u>your</u> words though. Hopefully they will explain it clearly to you so you understand.

3) They learned parenting from their parents. If something doesn't make sense, it may be because it was life-preserving 50 years ago. Again, no owner's manual and no automatic updates.

If you have moved out and are living on your own, and your parents are healthy, call them up to say "hi." Stop in at their house for no reason at all. Keep the communication open and share your joys and successes. All they've ever wanted for you was your success. Let them know they did okay.

If your parents are aging and need assistance, be there to help. You may not be able to do everything, and their needs may be beyond your skills. If it does become necessary to find a safer place, with professional help for your parents, then have that conversation and don't feel guilty about it. Keep in mind, this doesn't mean dropping them off and showing up on Mother's Day and their birthday. You have a responsibility to help them keep their spirit, and your presence will be very important as they are getting used to a new place and a new reality.

Siblings

Get together with your siblings from time to time whether it be a family gathering or lunch with just the two (or three or five) of you. Try not to get together with all but one sibling, unless there are only two or three of you. It feels too much like you're getting together to talk about him/her, unless you invite them and they just don't show up.

Watch the game together or have a barbecue. Keep the communication open. Compare notes on your parents' needs.

Support them through tough times, because you will need their support when you go through them as well. Care for them as you hope they will care for you.

Other relatives

This is a big category. You've got crazy uncles, quiet nieces, weird cousins and loud aunts. Laugh with them, cry with them.

At family gatherings, I recommend avoiding talking about politics. If your family can do so civilly, that is your call.

Don't bad-mouth their kids. Be supportive.

Keep communication lines open and be there when they need help.

You need to tailor your responses to each family member, no matter how strange they are. Keep things positive.

Good luck.

Family relationships are part of your life. For most of us, they always will be. How we interact with members of our family has a huge mental and emotional impact on who we are and what we do because their lives touch ours at so many points through many people. It is important to nurture these relationships when we can or limit them when necessary.

The better we understand these relationships, through our glasses, but also, as much as possible through their glasses, the better feel we will have for how our life design will be affected by family.

Step-by-Step

16. Are there any relationships that are in your top 10 priorities that are not as smooth as you wish they were? How might you address it?

Chapter 9

Friends and Acquaintances

*Friends are people who know you really well
and like you anyway.*

— Greg Tamblyn

Old Friends

Is there anything better? The kind of friend that you've known for so many years that they can complete your sentences for you. The nice thing about a friend this close is that good communication is easier. You've talked about everything for a long time, so it is difficult to surprise them. They've seen your ugly side, and they're still around.

Keep these kinds of friends close. Maintain your connection with them. Talk when you can. They will help you as you find your path and walk along it.

Then there are the newer friends. The ones you're just getting to know, or have only known for a little while. You don't have the history. They haven't seen how obnoxious you can be, so you may still be a bit reserved in these conversations. Treasure them. Work on them. Slowly open yourself up to them. Learn what makes them tick. Perhaps one day, they will become an "old friend."

*Set an example. Treat everyone with kindness
and respect, even those who are rude to you—not
because they are nice, but because you are.*

—Jonathon Lockwood Huie

Acquaintances

These could be people that you know that you have nothing in common with, so it is unlikely that you will become friends. These might be people with whom you used to have a connection, but you just don't have anything in common anymore. Perhaps it is someone you know who is a negative influence. In Chapter 18 we will talk a bit about time management, and in Chapter 4, we talked about priorities. You will have to determine where these people fit on your list.

It may sound a bit arrogant or even cruel, but you only have so much time in your day, so much time in your life. It is bad for your health to spend that time hanging around with people who bring you down and never bring you back up. Everyone gets down occasionally, sometimes even for long periods. Those may be people who need us to pour life into them and get them back on track. Don't ignore them. But, there are those who are happy being negative, and happiest when they are bringing others down. Don't do that to yourself. You don't have to call them names or be rude to them. Just be very careful about how much time, if any, you are going to spend near them.

*You are the average of the five people
you spend the most time with.*

— Jim Rohn

To a large extent, the people you hang around with determine your attitude. If you hang around with negative people, you will tend to be more negative, or at least have to work harder to be positive.

If you hang around with positive people, it will be easier to be optimistic about the world in general. Do be aware, there are positive people who will take you far away from your goals. Keep an eye on these relationships as it may require "re-centering" whenever you spend time with them. It doesn't mean they are bad, you just need to be aware of how they affect you.

If you spend too much time alone, you may lose track of the importance of others. You need others. I need others. We are not meant to be alone too much.

> *Life is too short to spend your precious time trying to convince the person who wants to live in gloom and doom otherwise.*
>
> — Zig Ziglar

Step-by-Step

17. Are there any associations in your life that are bad for you? What can you do about it?

Section III

DESIGN

Design v. To create, fashion, execute,
or construct according to plan[10]

You either build the life you want or accept whatever comes your way. The choice is entirely yours, but everyone will know what choice you have made.

If you want to live the life you were meant to live and not leave anything on the table when you are done, then you must figure out what that looks like and do the work to get there.

When an airplane takes off from Grand Rapids, Michigan, and is headed toward Dallas, Texas, the pilot does not point the nose of the plane at Dallas. She takes into account that the wind is blowing from west to east, so perhaps the nose of the plane is pointing toward Phoenix. During the flight, the direction and the intensity of the wind will change, and so the pilot adjusts the way the plane is pointing. The same is true as you design your life. Every step is designed to take you closer to your goal, and you make adjustments as you change and as the world around you changes.

---

[10] "design." *Merriam-Webster.com*. 2025. https://www.merriam-webster.com/dictionary/design (17 October 2025).

Designing your life isn't a "one and done" event. You need to do this process at least once a year. You change. The world changes. Your dreams change. Your purpose changes. The part you want to play in this world will change, too. Be open to it.

Getting the most out of life and not leaving any of it on the table comes down to planning it rather than just accepting it. And through the situation I found myself (described in the preface), I have been able to build a step-by-step process for doing just that. These are not original ideas; you can find them in many other books or speeches. This is just new packaging with my own house-blend of flavoring added.

The one thing I have found that seems to differ most with others I have encountered is step #1. Many writers and speakers indicate that step#1 is to figure out where you are. It is a valid place to start, but I have found that it limits your possibilities. Your mind will focus on things such as "I'm too old, or too young, or don't have the time, or can't afford it." When you begin with where you are, you bring with you all the baggage about who you are supposed to be and what you can't do. So, we start somewhere else.

The DESIGN framework is this:

Who do you wish you were? Step#1 is not the place to put on limitations—its the place to dream. When we're kids we want to be a fireman or doctor or circus clown ... it doesn't matter because nothing is off the table. Our whole world is ahead of us—nothing but possibilities.

Go there again. Dream. But don't limit it to careers. Really dream about every aspect of your life. There are many ways to do this. I recommend doing whatever works for you. Every new set of lenses you use will give you new insight.

Some possible methods (see the appendix for samples of each):

Cloud brainstorming—Write a central concept in the center of the paper and just keep branching out thought after thought.

Structured list—Write a concept, then write a sub-concept and a sub-sub-concept. You'll end up with something that looks like an outline of a book.

Just write—Take a clean sheet of paper and just start writing ideas all over the place as you think of them. Don't worry about where they fit; just write them down and keep writing until you have nothing else to write.

Any method that has worked for you—You may have some way that works for you that no one else uses. Then use that. This is about you and what works for you. Don't worry about whether someone likes your method or not.

After you know where it is you want to go, then you will need to figure out where you are starting from and the steps you will need to take to get to the future you want.

It is a process. Take each step seriously and be ready to do the work. If you're not sure what the best step is to take first, just pick something that you feel will get you moving in the right direction. Whatever you choose to do, you will learn something about what the next step will be.

WYSIWYG

There is an acronym in computer programming. WYSIWYG (pronounced wizzy-wig)

<u>W</u>hat

<u>Y</u>ou

<u>S</u>ee

<u>I</u>s

<u>W</u>hat

<u>Y</u>ou

<u>G</u>et

It basically means that what you see on the screen is what you will get on the printout or other output device.

An example would be a word processing program. You type letters that create words and sentences. You can see what you type on the screen. You change the fonts, put some in bold, some in italics. When it looks just right on the screen (What you see), you hit the print button, and the paper that prints (What you get) looks just like the screen.

WYSIWYG.

Life is a bit more complicated because there are two ways to see. You can see with your eyes, and you can see with your mind.

When you choose to be a victim in life, you see only with your eyes. You say to yourself, 'This is where I am. This is how I am made. This is how the people around me act. This is the hand I was dealt. This is how it will always be." And it will be. WYSIWYG.

But, unlike the word processor, you have the choice of seeing with your mind. All of the same stuff is there when you look with your eyes, but you don't end the thought with "This is how it always will be!" You continue on with" 'but what if ..." and your imagination takes over. You look at the things that aren't the way you want them to be—and you make a plan.

Every plan takes you further away from what you saw with your eyes and toward what you see in your mind—WYSIWYG.

If you want to see the power of the mind's eye, read the biography of Andrew Carnegie.

An extremely brief summary of his life:

- Born in poverty in Scotland
- Emigrated to the U.S. in 1848
- At age 13 worked from dawn to dusk in a cotton mill for $1.20 per WEEK
- Self-taught skills took him from each job to a better job.
- Had a goal to spend the first half of his life making money, which he did (inflation adjusted to over $300 billion (Carnegie Corporation)
- Had a goal to spend the second half of his life giving his money away (He was able to give away most of it, but ran out of time)
  - Funded 2509 libraries
  - Created the Carnegie Corporation to promote education and international peace (which is still operating today).

- Founded Carnegie Mellon University
- Much more ...

He saw what he wanted to do and did it.

When you decide that you can do better than you currently are, you also decide to put in the necessary work to achieve it. You will get what you see.

If you really desire to DESIGN the life you want, then you must put in the work. Are you ready to look at yourself closely? If so, then ...

... turn the page to begin.

You can do this.

Chapter 10

<u>D</u>ream

Dream: n. a cherished aspiration, ambition, or ideal

The future belongs to those who believe in the beauty of their dreams.

—Eleanor Roosevelt

Dream.

Weather-wise, it is a perfect day. Not cold and not hot. The sun is shining and there is a gentle breeze blowing.

For the first time in as long as you can remember, it is actually peaceful at home. Even the neighborhood seems to be resting. You hear some birds chirping. Even the occasional distant motor running seems to feel more calm than usual.

You are seated in your favorite seat, and your eyes slowly close, but not to sleep. Your mind is much too tuned into yourself for that.

You are amazed at what you see in your head. More clearly than ever before, you see your future.

It is incredible.

It is everything you've ever dreamed it would be. You see ...

What?

As you start getting a picture of what this looks like, begin writing it down. Don't worry about grammar, word choice, or even staying on any lines. Just write stuff down. IMPORTANT—While you are doing this exercise, do not think about your current life, limitations, duties, responsibilities, or whether anything in your dream is even possible (think of Spud Webb who, at 5' 7", won the NBA slam dunk" contest). We don't want to think about the present at this time because it will limit what we think about.

The universe is wide open to you in your dreams. Dream like a child does (astronaut, fireman, doctor ...). Just let it out and write it down. Write all over the page or pages. Every thought and idea.

I want to wear new shoes every day.

I want to have $10M in the bank.

I want to lose 10 pounds.

I want to live "off-grid."

I want to grow all my own food.

I want to give $1M to charity in a single year.

I want my kids and grandkids to be debt free.

I want everyone in my hometown to have opportunities to work.

I want to end homelessness in the county or state or country that I live.

I want to ride a unicycle.

I want to wear jeans every day.

I want to play running back in the NFL.

Write everything down and don't be neat about it. As long as you can read it, it's fine.

Got it all done?

Now wait a day. Think about it all overnight. The next day (or even a couple of days later) repeat the exercise, adding anything you missed. Don't worry if you repeat yourself. This is all for you, so no one else will see it. And it is better to list something twice than not at all.

Got that done? Are there any areas you missed describing? Where will you live? What sights have you seen? What languages will you know?

Okay—now you are confident you have everything. Right? If not, keep working on it. You want this as complete as is reasonable, but don't spend more than about a week. You will get all—or nearly all—of what you want in a week.

For a moment, we're going to step back to the present.

Look at the roles and priorities you developed earlier in the book. In your dreaming, did you describe the future of everything you listed as important to you? Each of your high priority ideas from Chapter 1 should have a future vision. If you missed one, then describe it now. If you realize that you missed it because it isn't really a priority, then go back and examine why you listed it as a priority in Section 1. There was something that caused you to write that down, understand what that reason is, and then figure out what you want that to look like in the future.

Okay, now you've got everything. This is your last chance to add to your dream. Just kidding, remember, I said you need to revisit this. Think of it as a living document that will change as you grow.

Now, you have your pages of brainstorming that describe your dream. Organize it a bit. I have found that list or a cloud-brainstorm works well here (you may know something that works better for you). I create a list or cloud for every main category. Work, Spouse, Children, Friends, Money, Charity, Home, Recreation, style—whatever makes sense based on your brainstorm.

Write down your dreams in a list. You will be using this list in the next step, so be complete. Use as many lists as you have categories with dreams. If one list gets long, break it into several. (For example: your list for family could get broken down to children, parents, siblings, shirttail or whatever).

Look at your lists. That should be a pretty good description of the life you want and are called to live. If you have any tweaks to make—go ahead.

So—does this list fire you up? If your life were like this, would it be easy to get up in the morning? If this doesn't fire you up, then keep dreaming. The fire is there somewhere.

We're getting close now. But we're not quite ready. You know yourself better than anyone else ... but you also have blind spots. So, let's solicit some help.

Find a friend or a relative who really wants you to succeed and who really knows you. Ask them this question (or one like it): "You've known me for a long time, and you've seen my ups and downs. You've heard me talk about my 'wishes and dreams', what things have I talked about most often as being important to me?"

I wouldn't ask this of any more than 5 people. When they answer you—think seriously about what they say. If it makes sense, and it isn't already on a list, then add it. If it doesn't make sense, then you might want to ask for some clarification so you can figure out what you have been saying or doing that gives that impression.

If you end up with a dream that doesn't seem to fit into a category, that's okay. Keep it on your list. You may find an underlying reason for it at some point. It may always be one of those things you want and don't know why, but I doubt it. There is probably a reason; it just may take some time to find it.

This should be a pretty good picture of where you want to go. Next, we will have to figure out where we are starting from, which brings us to the "E" in design.

Step-by-Step

Worksheets are available in the appendix or at www.theCoach.vip/SLLOT

18. Dream. Picture that perfect life and write down the details.

19. List major categories and what your dream is like in those categories.

Chapter 11

Examine

Examine: v. Inspect in detail to determine nature or condition

The examined life is the only life worth living.

— Socrates

The unexamined life may not be worth living, but the life too closely examined may not be lived at all.

— Mark Twain

Who do you think you are?!
I've heard that question more than once in my life. Usually from my mom. And I have to admit, it was a valid question nearly all the time.

But now, we're really going to look at who you think you are. You've had the fun and hard work of dreaming about your future. But we can't plan for the future without knowing the present, so you have to examine yourself now. Dig into how things really are, right now. Examine every area of your life, starting with the ones most important to you (the high priorities). The hard part of this is thinking objectively.

Remember, this is only for you, so be brutally honest. The clearer you are here, the better the next steps will work.

So, we begin with the facts. If you want to be real formal, you can—start with demographic data.

> My name is John, I'm a 58-year-old male living in West Michigan. My job titles are LifeCrafter, Speaker, and Author.

Go into as much detail as you want here. These are the easiest because they are objective.

The next part is breaking it into the roles. (see Chapter 3) For each of the roles you identified, give a brief narrative of the state of it.

> One of my roles is that of a member of my church. I have been an usher, a choir member, a praise team member, a Bible study leader, board member, Chairman of the Board, lawn care team member, youth leader, Financial Peace University leader and many other roles. As of the writing of this book, I am in the choir and praise team. I also occasionally serve as an advisor to various ministry leaders (all of whom are extremely capable on their own). I attend worship on average once a week. I support the church financially. I have a 25-30 minute commute to my church and have been attending the same congregation since 1978, which is also where and

when I met my wife. I currently spend about 2 hours per week travelling to and from church activities and events.

That is my current summary of that role. Do this with every role you hold. It can be written out as I did, or it can be bulleted :

- Role.—Church Member
- Praise Team
- Choir
- Advisor
- Longtime Member
- Long commute.
- Etc.

After you have gone through all your roles, think about any important areas of your life that maybe don't fit into a specific role. These should be limited, but you may have one or two.

When you are confident that you have everything, then look at your dream list of your perfect future. Do you have an 'examination' of the present state for all the future items? If not, then write those now. Remember, this is all judgment-free. Each item should be accurate whether you are proud of it or not. You won't have to share this with anyone.

So, what do we do with this information? Turn the page and find out

Step-by-Step

Worksheets are available in the appendix or at www.theCoach.vip/SLLOT

20. Examine. Do you have a current state listed for every dream listed?

Chapter 12

State the Difference

Have you ever watched Bob Ross paint? He takes a blank canvas and throws paint at it for 20 minutes and ends up with something beautiful.

On his show it appears that he is adding elements at random, but he isn't. He has a plan. He already knows what the final painting will look like. Maybe a brush or rock is different, but it is mostly determined ahead of time.

So he knows what the end is, a beautiful waterfall in the forest. He knows what the beginning is, a blank white canvas. Just like you know what you want and what your future looks like and what your present looks like.

Now Bob knows that the canvas is blank, and he needs to have a tree in the corner. There needs to be some mountains on the top left. There are lots of rocks to be placed.

He is determining what is different from the current canvas to his future vision.

You have looked at your future and figured out what you want it to look like. You've also looked at your current life "warts and all."

Now it is time to figure out where things are out of alignment or not yet achieved.

If you are not using the worksheets from the appendix, the easiest way to see this is by making a quick chart with 3 columns. (The worksheets in back follow a process, so the "State the Difference" page combines columns 1 and 2 as described here.)

The first column is what you found when you examined your current life. This is what IS.

The second column is where you write your dreams. What WILL BE.

In the third column you will compare the two. How are they different? Get into the details here. Don't be judgmental. These differences are the facts and the starting point for improvement. So if you are looking at your time spent with kids and you currently spend about 10 minutes a day (Column 1) and you want to spend an hour a day (Column 2) then you would write something like—"In order to spend 60 minutes a day with my kids, I will need to increase the time I currently spend by 50 minutes each day."

Time spent with kids

Current condition	Dreamed condition	How is it different
10 minutes a day	60 minutes a day	The dream is 50 minutes greater per day

Do not try to figure out how you can do this. That question is for later. Right now, you're just figuring out *what* needs to be done, not *how* to do it.

Some of these will be a little tricky to figure out the wording. The struggle will help you understand it better, so don't shy away from it.

You will do this for every dream or role or goal. Whatever you want to change. Take your time and do it well. You will use this in the next area as you start designing your plan.

At this point, you and Bob Ross know what is missing ... what's the best way to add it ...

Step-by-Step

Worksheets are available in the appendix or at www.theCoach.vip/SLLOT

21. State the differences between the future and the present.

Chapter 13
Ideate

Ideate v. form an idea of; imagine or conceive

Idea generation is about quantity, not quality.
Multiplication, not subtraction. Editing comes later.
The goal of brainstorming is to walk out with buckets
of ideas, not one precious idea perched on a pillow.

— Sam Harrison, *Creative Zing!*

I have to admit it—this one is my favorite.
Generating ideas, options, for how to get from Point A to Point B is right up my alley. Your goal here is to find options to get from your "NOW" to your "WILL BE." This is another one of those brainstorming things, so have fun with it. Don't make any choices here. Just generate ideas. Make sure you have at least three ideas (preferably many more) for every item that you want to change (From "Now" to "Dream"). Think outside the box!

Once again, don't be constrained by logical or even possible. Throw everything against the wall and see what sticks.

In our example of my role as a member of my church, I noted that I have a 30-minute drive to and from church. This could limit the ways I could be involved because there is only so much time in the day. So, what are some ways I can deal with that? Let's brainstorm.

1. Nothing. Just accept it.

2. Move—Sell my house and buy one closer to the church

3. Buy a condo or rent an apartment near the church for the busy times of week

4. Try to get everything I want to be involved with to happen on the same day

5. Convince the church to buy a new building closer to me

6. Only participate virtually. Use phone calls and video meetings.

7. Host some meetings at my house.

8. Drive Faster

I created this list in less than 10 minutes. Imagine what could be done in an hour. What other ideas can you come up with for my example? Try to think of at least two.

The point here is to look at every possibility, no matter how outrageous. The more things you have listed, the more likely you will be able to generate a good plan. It may be one of them on your list. More likely, it will be a combination of ideas.

Invite friends. Don't be afraid to ask others to help you brainstorm ideas. Just make sure they understand, this is not the time to evaluate, just generate ideas.

A word of caution, or perhaps of anticipation—this may turn into multiple paths that you wish to pursue. I have a dream to write a book. This showed up in the Dream portion of my planning, but I had nothing in my present situation (Examine) to start with, so the path was wide open. I ended up with multiple paths that lead to multiple books. The one you are reading now is the first one.

Step-by-Step

Worksheets are available in the appendix or at www.theCoach.vip/SLLOT

22. Generate as many ideas as possible to bridge the gap between now and future.

Chapter 14
Game Plan

You've generated lots of ideas for each of your paths. Now you need to choose one. Don't dismiss things too quickly, unless they violate your beliefs. Evaluate them one at a time and look at the steps that you would need to take—just at a high level.

So, in our example:

1. Do nothing. This is always an option. Whether or not it is viable depends on how big the problem is that you are trying to solve. In this case, a 30-minute commute is a little annoying, especially during the winter, but it isn't earth-shattering.

2. Move. Sell my house and move closer. My wife and I love our house and the setting. We had chosen it because it was away from city noise, and the floor plan is one that will hopefully work fine for the rest of our lives.

   Selling the house would be an "extreme negative" for my wife, and because she is one of my highest priorities, then it would be a negative for me. This is a "No."

3. Buy a condo or rent an apartment near the church. Right off the bat this seems like a big hassle. Maintaining two homes is expensive. Would my wife

spend those nights there too, or would she stay at the main house? What nights would I spend there? This stresses me out just thinking about it. It's a "No."

4. Try to get everything I want to do happening on the same day. This one has possibilities, so let's think through the steps a bit more. What tasks do I want to be involved in? When do they meet? Who is in charge of those things and are they open to changing times/ dates? How many people would this effect? What day(s) would be best for me? For them? There are a lot of questions here, but it might be workable. This is a "maybe."

5. Convince the church to buy a building near to me. This one isn't completely off the table, though it seems silly. What if the church has outgrown its facilities (or it has shrunk to a point where most of the building is empty most of the time)? Maybe there is a perfect sized building available right near me. Maybe the church mortgage is too big and selling to buy something cheaper is smart planning. Perhaps the church is considering a satellite building. In our situation, none of these are true at this time, so, for now, this is a "no."

6. Only participate virtually. The world has changed greatly since 2020. Virtual meetings happen all the time. Could this work for me? Well, Bible studies could, advising could, readings during worship is a stretch, but we already have virtual worship, so it is possible, but we lose out on a lot of fellowship opportunities, preaching is an even bigger stretch, but there are some local churches that operate that way.

Choir and Praise Team ... well, there's a problem. I don't think we have enough people with good enough equipment or fast enough internet to make this work. Maybe with a lot of expense ...

So, this one is partially workable.

7. Host some meetings at my house. This is viable for some aspects, including Praise Team, Choir, advising, and Bible Studies. The rest of them would be a problem—unless we did those virtually. This one would require a lot of work and would also increase the driving time for everyone else involved. This one doesn't look too good.

8. Drive faster. My car is capable of going faster than I ask her to go. However, I have seen what excess speed on public roads can do. Lives can change in an instant. I also have a belief that all just laws should be obeyed—so this option would violate that one. That makes this a "no."

As you can see, this can really be enlightening. Some really strange ideas may actually be the best.

Also, as you evaluate each of these, you generate other ideas. Don't be afraid of that. Write them down and think about them.

Now choose your path. You will put in some of the details here, but the nitty-gritty will be done in the next step. As it turns out, I think the best path for me involves a combination of several of these.

I believe my best path is

- Continue living where I do

- Conduct the advising over the phone or virtually or when I'm already at church
- Conduct Bible Studies virtually or at a time when I'll already be at church
- Try to coordinate choir & praise team to be on the same day or on days when I am already there
- Evaluate any new opportunities that come up and make sure they are aligned with my principles, priorities, goals and schedule. Say 'no' if they aren't.

This practical example and best path does not have a lot of "step-by-step," but here is where you would do that. For the sake of an example, let's pretend that my ideal path was #2 above. Sell my house and move closer. (Don't tell my wife.)

How will that happen? Break it into steps. Some people like to take steps forward, from now to later. Some like to do them backward, starting with the end and work backward for the steps. I have found it works best to just put the steps down on paper in random order at first. Get all the steps that I know need to happen out there. I then put them in the order they need to happen and also fill in between steps if they are "too big."

So, I have my current house. I'm going to sell it and buy a new house, or maybe a condo. Assuming my wife agrees, then we will need to do the following things:

- Decide on House or Condo
- How close do we need to be to church?
- Sell the house ourselves or hire a professional realtor?
- Deep clean the house

- Find a new place
- Get all the extra boxes and furniture out of our existing house and into storage
- Put a sign in the yard

There are a lot more steps, but we'll use these for the example. Now we put them in order:

1. Do we want a house or a condo?
2. How close do we need to be to church?
3. Decide whether we will sell it ourselves, or use a realtor
4. Get all the clutter out of the house and into storage
5. Deep clean
6. Find a new place
7. Put a sign in the yard

When we decide to use a Realtor in #3, then we will have to add

3.0 Will we sell ourselves, or use a realtor?

3.1 Interview Realtors

3.2 Choose a realtor

Each decision we make will clarify our next steps. We figure out some steps ahead of time, and then add other steps, or remove them as we move toward that final goal.

We do this process each time we're planning a goal.

The next step is probably the most important of all.

Step-by-Step

Worksheets are available in the appendix or at www.theCoach.vip/SLLOT

23. Game Plan. Choose the steps to get from 'now' to 'dream.' Especially the first step.

24. Repeat steps 19–21 for every dream.

Chapter 15

<u>N</u>ow, Do It!

A dream doesn't become reality through magic; it takes sweat, determination, and hard work.

— *Colin Powell*

T here is no "JUST" about it.
Doing it takes commitment. Commitment can be hard.

This is the most important step in this process. Do it. Begin!

And don't do it eventually, <u>Do it Now</u>!

You are usually far better off doing something now, with just a little thought on what you are going to do, then you would be to wait until you had a perfect plan ready. Here's a secret ... You will never have a perfect plan ready. NEVER.

And how does a plan you never execute help you?

Through the past few chapters, you have already put more time into the design than most people ever do. So put the rubber to the road and see where it takes you. You may have to make some adjustments, maybe even ask for directions along the way. But you will be closer to your designed future than you were when you started.

When you've gotten past the first step or two, make any adjustments needed. When you are walking through unfamiliar territory, you can only see 20 feet in front of you, then walk 10 feet and have a look around. You'll be able to see 10 feet further than when you started. It's the same in life. The further you go, the further you can see.

It's kind of like Sudoku. I find them very enjoyable. If you've never done them, they are a simple 9x9 grid. The 9x9 grid is also broken down into 9 3x3 grids. You are given a few numbers to begin with, randomly scattered through the puzzle and you have to fill in the rest. When complete, you will have numbers 1–9 represented in each row, column, and 3x3 box. That's it.

You start with what you know and use logic to figure out what comes next. Every time you figure out where a number goes, it gives you a little bit more information about where the next one will go. It is the same with your plan. As you move forward, you have a little bit more information and a little better idea of your next step.

Which One?

So, which of your plans should you do first? Remember earlier in the book when you prioritized your roles and goals? This is where you use that. You should focus on the highest priority tasks/goals. One or two of them. Three is the absolute most that I would recommend.

Don't forget to consider goals that may be important in reaching the high priority goals.

If you have a goal to be married, and an even higher goal of having kids, and you also have a value of "no sex outside of marriage," then you will either need to put your lower priority goal (marriage) ahead of your higher priority goal (children). Or perhaps you could adopt.

And, as always, keep in mind the priorities of the people who are most important to you. What is important to them is important to you because it is important to them.

So pick a couple and get moving ...

It's your life—DESIGN it!

Step-by-Step

Worksheets are available in the appendix or at www.theCoach.vip/SLLOT

    25. Now, Do it! Start now with step 1.

Chapter 16

Summarize

You've just gone through a long process of figuring out what you want in the future and how to get there.

You know the first steps you need to take in the areas of your life that need the first changes. And you have taken those first steps.

Now you have to keep the momentum.

Consider telling a friend or finding someone who will keep you accountable to your goals.

As you complete steps in your plan, you can see a little further so you can do your next steps. When things are rolling well, perhaps you add in another one of your plans/goals. The idea is to be constantly moving in the direction of the life you want and are meant to have.

Add new goals as they are revealed to you. Eliminate the ones that are no longer relevant. Keep growing and make minor adjustments as you go.

You can do this.

Dream about your ideal future

Examine your current situation

State the Differences

Ideate the Options

Game Plan—Choose an option

Now Do it!—Do step #1 today

> *Q. When is the best time to plant a tree?*
> *A. Twenty years ago.*

> *Q. When is the second-best time to plant a tree?*
> *A. Today*

> *— Ancient proverb*

Section IV

DESIGN Application

O kay, we've gone through a lot. The "fixer" in me can't just leave it here.

The point of this book is to give you hope and help you find direction and purpose. I hope what you've read so far is doing that for you.

There are a few topics that people ask me about frequently. These appear to be important enough that, if left unresolved, will get in the way of DESIGNing your perfect life.

In order to prevent these from getting in the way of your DESIGN process, I want to highlight them and supply some thoughts about dealing with them.

Everyone's situations are different, so these may or may not apply to you. You also may not agree with me. That's okay.

If you are doing something different than I talk about on any of these questions, and it is working for you, don't stop! I do not have all the answers, and you know you better than I.

However, if what you've been doing isn't working then you either need to accept the results you've been getting or do something different.

Chapter 17
Attitude

Whether you think you can, or you think you can't—you're right.

— Henry Ford

There may be nothing that affects your life and your success more than your attitude. These beliefs about yourself, your life, and the world around you will affect your actions and how you perform them. Your attitude is your choice.

Optimist or pessimist

Do you expect the best will happen or the worst will happen? I used to say I was a realist, neither optimist or pessimist. I've since come to believe that there is no such thing as a realist. In order to truly be a realist, you have to know the future, and we can't. We have an expectation of what will happen, and that may be good or bad or even middle of the road. But we don't know. So, which are you going to believe?

I'm a big fan of optimism. I believe that generally, things are going to work out all right. Am I disappointed sometimes? Sure, I don't always get what I want. But I find that I am more likely to get the things I think about, so I choose to think about the things I want.

Scarcity or abundance

A scarcity mentality says that there is only so much to go around, an abundance mentality says that the amount available can increase as the need increases. I believe that the world has far more available to us than we will ever be able to use. You don't have to take from others to get what you want or need. You can both have everything you need.

> *You can have everything in life you want, if you just help other people get what they want.*
>
> — Zig Ziglar

There is plenty for everyone.

Responsible or victim

Are you going to take responsibility for your situation or blame others for it? Bad things happen to us. It may or may not be your fault. However, it is your responsibility to deal with the situation and grow from it. The other option is to blame someone else and get stuck there.

Either way, the bad thing happened. Are you going to sit there and suffer, or are you going to take the adversity as something to learn from and build something from it?

It's a choice.

But I Don't Feel Like it! (Perseverance)

If you do everything in this book and consistently follow all the steps—and do it every day—you'll be in good shape. You will no longer be leaving life on the table.

But you know as well as I do, there are days you just don't feel like it.

You don't even feel like goofing off. You don't want to do anything.

I get it. I have that too. In fact, this chapter is being written because I spent the last couple of days moping around the house not accomplishing much of anything. I just didn't feel like it.

After all, no one will buy my book anyway. And if they did buy it, they wouldn't learn anything because I put it together wrong. The outline doesn't make sense. And my office is messy. It's hot outside.

Now for a guy who has decided that his purpose in life is to help people find and achieve their purpose, several days of sucking my thumb was more than enough.

So, I'm here to tell you from experience, when this happens to you, and it will, there is a way to get out of that funk.

First, recognize that it will happen from time to time. Don't beat yourself up over it. Acknowledge that it is true and give yourself permission to step away and do whatever you may want to do—guilt free.

Don't live there though. Just visit. When you've blown off a little stress, look at your purpose and goals. Recall your

"Why." Is it still valid? It probably is. If your "why" is strong enough, it will get you through. A short spate of "the grumps" isn't usually a sign that you're on the wrong path. *It usually means that you need to do a little personal maintenance.*

Once you've given yourself a little time to refresh—then jump back in. Grab hold of that one single most important item that you want to do next—and do it!

It's important to start back with one thing, the most important thing. This will help you get re-centered and back on track.

If this doesn't get you moving in the right direction, then ask someone for help. You may just need to vent to a friend. You might need to reach out to a coach or a therapist. And in case you are wondering, I have all three, friends, a coach and a therapist. I am thankful for them all.

There is no shame in seeking help. You can't do it all on your own.

Being Tired

We all get tired. Life can be exhausting.

As I write this, I am 58 years old. I've raised two children, worked at a company for a quarter of a century, including 10+ years as CEO. I served as a Music Minister in the United States, Australia, and Papua New Guinea, did short-term ministry in Guatemala; Houston, Texas; and Grand Rapids, Michigan. I was on the Church Council/Business Council/Board of Directors for more than 20 Years—7 of them as the Chairman. The list of things that I have done, successfully and unsuccessfully, is long.

You have a long list of things you have done too. If the list isn't as long as mine, it is probably because I am older than you. Maybe a lot older than you!.

With all the demands we have on us, we have the right to be tired sometimes. That doesn't mean we have to sit in a chair and watch the world.

60 is the new 40.

I remember when I was younger, watching people in their 50's winding down on physical activity. "I'm too old. I'll break a hip."

Well, that just isn't true anymore. My older brother still plays soccer multiple times every week. My father is in his mid-80's and golfs many times every week. I don't see either of them stopping those activities anytime soon.

We are not made to sit still. When we do, our bodies begin dying. When we stay active our bodies keep working. Like a car that is driven every day compared to one that sits in a barn and is never used. It will rust out.

That's true of our minds as well. Sitting in a recliner, filling your brain with the latest wisdom from a sitcom will not keep your brain humming along in high gear. (It is a great diversion—but shouldn't be the whole day)

If like me, you are tired from all the demands on your life and all the abuse you're taken. Wear those "been there, done that" badges with pride and go look for some more.

And if you want to take an hour nap every day—do it! There are entire countries that have been doing that for centuries.

And if 5-year-olds need nap time—then its okay for you and I too.

As the old saying goes, 'your attitude determines your altitude.' Keeping your attitude positive can be tough—especially when you are tired. When your attitude is in the dumps, take note of it, and see if you can figure out why. This is tough, but can be very beneficial.

Chapter 18

Time Management

In this life, time is our most precious commodity. When you are born, you're given a certain number of days to live. You can't get any more. You can't save it. You can't trade it. You can't buy it.

All you can do is use it. You have to decide how. Every choice you make means that you can't use that time for anything else. In business, this is called the "opportunity cost."

You can't do everything (I'm really weak on this one). You have to budget your time just like you budget your money.

Choose wisely, because unlike money, you can't make any more.

Time Management

When I think of time management, I always think of my mom. She didn't have any formal training on how to get stuff done; she just *knew* how to get stuff done. I can picture her every morning. Sitting at the dining room table, a cup of black coffee in front of her, a cigarette in one hand (she quit when I was in high school), and a yellow-barreled Bic pen in the other. She had a small notepad, spiral bound on top.

On the top line, she wrote the day of the week, and under it was her "To-Do List." She just wrote down everything she had to get done that day. When she finished an item, she crossed it off. When she did something that wasn't on her list, she wrote it on her list and then crossed it off. Giving herself "credit" for everything she did gave her more motivation to keep getting stuff done.

When I was in college, I had a job as a manager at Burger King. At that time, my brother Jeff was my boss. He introduced me to the Franklin Planner. A fantastic tool which helped me to prioritize my daily, weekly, and monthly goals. I have always found time management to be fascinating (yeah, that's one of the many ways I'm a bit weird), and I learned many different methods that work for many different people. What I use now is my own combination of numerous methods.

The key to time management is not which method you use but having a method and using it. However, I have always found that my best time usage results came when I looked not only at what "needed" to be done, but also at what is important to me. By knowing what matters to me, I make sure those things get done and then I fit the other things around them. Remember the jar we introduced earlier? It gives us an image of both our life's priorities and our ability to manage our time. If you start your day with water, some rocks are bound to be left out, and you'll have a mess on the table. The same is true in life. If you fill your day with things that are important to you (the rocks) then you will still have time for things of lesser importance, but even if you don't, you still accomplish those things that are most important to you.

If you fill your day with things that don't matter—then you never have the feeling of accomplishment—you never feel like your life matters.

Learning about and doing those things that are most important to you makes all the difference. Does this mean you always do "your stuff" and ignore everyone else? Not at all. Keep in mind, if someone is important to you, then what is important to them is also important to you. So if your best friend is heavily involved with feeding the world, then supporting him/her in that should be important to you, even if you don't have a passion for feeding the world.

The same is true for work. If your family is important to you, then doing a good job at work should be important to you so that they have food to eat and a place to live. If feeding the world is an important cause for you, then contributing to that cause will be important to you. That's really all there is to it.

Find a system that works for you to make sure you are getting the important things done.

We spent a lot of time figuring out what was important to you earlier in this book. This is where you figure out how to use it on a daily basis.

Keep in mind, we only get a certain amount of time to work with. When the sand runs out, you can't turn the hourglass over. We also have no idea how much time we have left. So we plan like we have lots of time left and live like today is our last day. Plan for the worst, hope for the best.

Another important thing to keep in mind; don't schedule every moment of your day. Keep some time open for emergencies and for just not having something to do. I'm not good at this, but much better than I used to be. I used to schedule my day from 5:30AM – 10:00PM in 15-minute increments. The whole day. Everything was full. If something came up, I had to reschedule something or everything.

Leave some gaps in your schedule. If possible, allocate a little extra time for projects to cover the unexpected things that come up. Because they *will* come up.

Also, include larger gaps where you give yourself time to do, "whatever you darn well please." This could be a walk with your dog, coffee with your spouse, video games, hobbies, whatever you feel like doing at that moment.

This is in addition to the time you may have specifically scheduled for that purpose. You need time that isn't earmarked for anything. It's good for your soul to just breathe sometimes.

Daily Goals & Routine

Make a list of things you do every week on specific days. This will help you to never forget them, and will also keep you from worrying about things on off-days. For example, if you do laundry on Tuesday, then you don't have to think about it on the other days. You'll do it on Tuesday.

Some items may show up on several days' lists. When raising a family, laundry can easily be Monday, Wednesday, and Friday.

One last thing on time usage, Don' t multi-task. Do one thing and then do the other. When "multi-tasking," you are most likely actually "switching." Going back and forth from one thing to another, not actually doing them at the same time. So you are actually wasting time having your brain switch directions so often. You'll be much more efficient just taking things in order. Prioritize them, then do them.

The Myth of Work/Life balance.

I hear many people tell me they are looking for work/life balance. There is no such thing. There is just balance.

Your work is part of your life. Do you say you are looking for sleep/life balance? I've never heard it.

We want balance. True life balance is kind of a weird thing and hard to nail down because it is constantly changing. It may be that you spend 12 hours a day, 7 days a week at work. That's half of your life. Is that in balance? Maybe. What makes up the other 50%?

What is life? Is life, sleeping, eating, traveling, reading, watching TV, spending time with friends/family/children/God—all in whatever percentage mix we want? Is there a golden ratio?

When someone retires and quits working, are they now out of balance for the rest of their life?

Let me give you a new definition of balance to try on for size.

Balance is the allocation of time and energy that most efficiently moves you toward all of your desired outcomes.

This definition of balance allows us to change how we are using our time based on the current needs of our goals. There are times in our life when certain goals take a back-seat to other goals, by DESIGN. That doesn't make other goals less important; they just might need less time temporarily.

Some possible examples:

- When you have children in high school, they will need more of your time than they will when they have moved out

- When you first start a business, your work will require more time than it will later when it is running smoothly

- If you have an ailing parent, your time with them may increase

- If your doctor tells you that if you don't lose 20 pounds, you're going to have a heart attack, then your exercise time may increase

- If you have a woodworking hobby, and you're making a present for someone, your hobby time may increase

There are infinite mixes of how you spend your time, based on your needs/priorities for the day. I don't know what your priorities are. Only you can determine what your time mix should be at any given moment, but don't be afraid to ask others for input. Fresh eyes can be very helpful.

Planning your days and weeks, prioritizing the order you do things, spending an appropriate amount of time on things are all an integral part of DESIGNing your life. You have figured out what is important to you (values, roles, goals, and people) and you are now setting aside the time to focus on the tasks you need to accomplish in order to move from the present you to the future you.

Chapter 19
Money

For the love of money is a root of all kinds of evils.

— I Timothy 6:10 ESV

Money is not the root of all evil. There is nothing wrong with money. The love of money is the root of all kinds of evil. When you place money above other people or above your values and beliefs, you will run into problems. There is nothing wrong with earning money. We need it to buy the things that we need. We need it to buy the things that we want. We need it to help others in many ways. Do not let others make you feel guilty if you are making a good living.

Money is a tool. Money in and of itself is useless. You can't eat it, you can't drink it, it won't love you back. I suppose it could keep you warm for a little while if you burn it. Don't try to accumulate money for the sake of having it. If you are going to accumulate it—do so with purpose, and make sure it aligns with your values and principles. This use of money helps us to not leave life on the table. Think about which of your goals or values requires money; that's the end goal, the money isn't.

How we use money is important and can be looked at similar to how we use our time. It is limited, and we need to use it where we want to use it.

I am not going to go through a full personal finance plan here. That isn't the purpose of this book. There are a couple of pointers I will share. These are my opinions, and not everyone will agree with me. There are wealthy people who follow everything I'm about to say and there are wealthy people who don't do any of them. Also, please remember that your definition of wealth doesn't need to include vast sums of money.

Budgeting

The plans of the diligent lead surely to abundance,
but everyone who is hasty comes only to poverty.

— Proverbs 21:5 ESV

I believe the single most important thing you can do to create and protect wealth is to have a budget. Many people don't like having a budget because they feel that it is their money and they should be allowed to spend it however they want. I agree with that thought.

A budget is precisely that. Spending your money however you want. Where you *really* want. Not spending it on a whim that you will regret later.

A budget is telling your money where to go instead
of wondering where it went.

— Dave Ramsey

Have you ever had that time when you looked in your wallet and saw a $5 bill and thought to yourself that you were sure you had a $20? What happened?

That other $15 went to a candy bar, a fountain drink, and the latest magazine on your hobby. Is there anything wrong with that? No, it's your money. But that $15 today and tomorrow and a few more days like it will keep you from being able to take the vacation you've been saving up for, or from replacing the old clunker with something a little newer, or possibly from paying rent.

Make a budget. Even if it is just a simple one. If you're married, work on it together.

There are many apps that help you create a budget. You can find them for free. You can also do it on paper very easily. I've included a sheet in the appendix, which is also available on the website www.theCoach.vip/SLLOT.

Take a blank sheet of paper. On the left side you write down all the money you know you will take in this month—this your income. Add it up.

On the right side, you write down all the things you know you will spend money on in this month. First you write down the "Must pays." I believe the first item here should be charity. (There are many reasons for this, but you'll need to make this decision for yourself.)

On the "musts," you will include any debt payments (you promised to pay this back), any basic life costs: food (not restaurants), shelter, utilities (including phone & internet) You also need to include, soap, detergent, clothing, gas and oil changes for the car, taxes, insurance, doctor/dentist, etc. All the stuff that needs (not wants) to be paid every month. If you don't remember everything, look at your bank statement for the past three months and see where you've been spending it.

Don't forget, you need to set aside money for emergencies and for retirement!

Add this all up.

You will now subtract the "Must pay" total from the "income" total.

If the "must pay" is higher than the income, something needs to change. You're going backward, and unlike the government, you can't do that forever.

You will either need to make more money or change some spending habits.

If the "must pay" is lower than the income, then you have what is called "discretionary income." (Not "disposable income." Who came up with that term?) That is money you can spend on wants. This could be a vacation, a house, a new car, whatever. But budget it and save up for it. Buy it when you have the money saved.

Create a new budget every month because your income and expenses change every month. Be aware that the first few budgets will be terrible. Keep doing it. It will get easier, and you will get more accurate.

Debt

There are those who believe that you can maximize your financial position by borrowing as much money as possible and using other people's money to make more money. As a general rule I disagree with this idea. When we are in debt to other people, there is always some degree of stress, some degree of anxiety, over what would happen if we suddenly couldn't pay our bills. When we don't use debt, then we are less vulnerable to changes in pricing and society as a whole.

There are some things that may require debt. A home mortgage is one. These days, a car may be another but do that carefully. Perhaps student loans, but there are ways to avoid having large college loans.

Remember that paying back loans is not optional. You promised you would pay it back and your integrity requires you to do so. Don't listen to those financial gurus that talk about taking loans in some fancy way so you won't be liable if you default. That's just wrong.

4 Mistakes People Make When Getting Out of Debt

Avoiding Creditors—If you have a debt that you are having trouble repaying, call the creditor and let them know. They may not help at all, but if you are straight with them about your situation, they will typically work with you to figure out a way to get the debt paid. It is in their best interest to help you, after all, they want to get paid.

Focusing on the Forest—If you have a lot of debt, it is natural to look at everything that you owe and be overwhelmed. Don't do that. Be aware of your debts, and if possible, make at least the minimum payment on each one. But, focus on one debt and pay it off before you pay anything beyond the minimum on the other debts.

Focusing on interest rates—Mathematically, it makes sense to pay off the highest interest rate debt first. However, debt doesn't tend to be a math problem. It is an attitude or an education problem. You need to build some successes in money management and also limit the number of items distracting you, so I recommend paying off the smallest one first. Ignore the interest rate as it really doesn't make that much of a difference. If you have two debts that are the same, then look at the interest rate.

Borrowing money to pay off debts—I played the "get a new zero percent interest rate on balance transfer" game. It just gets you deeper in the hole. If you are having a problem with debt, taking on more debt is not the solution. Turn down your spending, don't increase debt. (Remember, you are not the federal government.)

Credit Cards

I'll gladly pay you Tuesday for a hamburger today.

— Wimpy from *Popeye*

I'm not a fan of credit cards. Think of it this way: Whenever you use a credit card, you are taking out a loan for whatever you bought.

Do you really want a bank loan for an energy drink and a donut?

Credit Cards make it too easy to ignore your budget. Avoid them when you can. Consider a debit card if you need the convenience. For those of you who must have a credit card for emergencies, keep it to one card with a low limit. No more than $5000, and that's pushing it.

If you have had problems with credit card debt in the past, then avoid them altogether now. It's a hard habit to break.

Wants versus Needs

Wants versus needs is a very important concept. I think my kids grew very tired of hearing me talk about it. But it is an essential concept for contentment and for financial stability.

The idea of a need is something you must have to live. You must have food. You must have shelter. You must have heat in the winter (if you live somewhere that has a real winter).

You may want a steak, but you don't need a steak, you need food.

You may want Nike Air Jordans. But you don't need Nike Air Jordans. You need shoes.

You may want a 10-bedroom mansion on 500 acres in the mountains of Tennessee. But you just need a place to live which could be a mobile home in a community.

When I was in Papua New Guinea I became acquainted with a young man who told me that he really needed a watch. Maybe things have changed, but when I was there, no one needed a watch. Events would be at "5 o'clock *sumting*" (This means anywhere between 5:00 and 7:00.) A watch was a status symbol, a luxury. Certainly not a need.

Sometimes wants and needs are hard to differentiate. They are also not the same for each person. I don't need a pair of steel-toed work boots. For me, they might be a want. My brother-in-law works in construction, so for him steel-toed work boots are a need.

Don't get caught in the race against the people around you to be sure you have newer, bigger and better things than they do.

Also, remember to watch out for the marketing ploy of 'you deserve this.' If you've set up a reward for yourself, then go ahead. But you don't need some big reward for everything you do.

Set up your priorities and make your purchases according to what really is important to you.

Be true to where you are

If you are shopping for a large ticket item—do not even look at options above the price. you determined ahead of time that you can afford. I learned this from my sister-in-law.

If you are looking for a house and have determined you can afford $300,000—don't look at a $500,000 house just to get ideas. It will make you dissatisfied with what you can afford. That takes the fun out of the purchase or makes you spend more than you can afford to spend. This leads to stress down the road.

Be content with what you can do now. If something grander is important to you, then build a plan (DESIGN) to get there.

Chapter 20
Health

Take care of yourself. Your mind and your body.
If something goes wrong with it, where will you live?

Do you want to increase the time you have available? Then take care of yourself. All aspects of yourself.

You need to take care of your body, mind, and spirit.

Physical Health

We'll start with body since it is the easiest to examine. We can get all sorts of measurements and tests. Visit your doctor regularly.

I've struggled with one aspect of my health for my entire life. As of the writing of this. book, I'm working my way to my ideal weight (this is not the government-suggested weight. The only time I was at that weight was when I had a tropical disease—it was bad). Working with my doctor I have chosen a target weight. By the time this book is published, I will be there. Go ahead and ask me.

Getting to an appropriate weight requires eating and sleeping well and getting exercise. That can be whatever you want— just get that body moving. Find a diet that works for you.

"Diet" only means the mix of foods you're eating. There are lots of different ones available. Do your research or hire someone to help you. If you hire someone, do your research when you choose.

And sleep!

I hear so many people brag about how little sleep they get or need. Studies show that as adults we need 6-8 hours of sleep. The exceptions are extremely rare. When we get less than 6 hours (for me it is 7 1/2), we have more time to work, but we get less done. We are much less productive. Our brains need to rest.

Play!

Have some fun.

> *All work and no play makes Jack a dull boy.*
>
> —Jack Torrence from *The Shining*

It makes you dull, and sick too. When you have fun you may exercise your body, or your mind, or refresh your spirit, or all of these.

Have you ever been working on a project where nothing is going right? Perhaps someone has approached you and invited you to go do something fun. You decide to go along with it because you aren't really accomplishing anything anyway. You go away, have fun, and then you come back to the project. By some miracle, now it all makes sense and works together nicely. Sometimes your brain just needs to change direction.

In addition to exercise, you can maintain and even improve the health of your spirit by sitting quietly. Our society seems to be built on noise. There's always something bombarding us for attention.

Turn off the TV/Computer/Phone/Radio. Sit quietly, breathe deeply and just think or even talk to God. Don't worry about the world around you. They're all just fine for the few minutes you're going to be doing this.

Mental Health

There are many dimensions to your mental health. You can improve your mental health by reading, talking with friends, sharing stories around a campfire, meditating and prayer. You can learn skills for dealing with stress from books, lectures or a professional therapist. Don't neglect your mental health because if your mind and spirit aren't working well, nothing else will.

In this realm is also your artistic side. I believe everyone has one and you need to let it out from time to time. It might be painting, or woodworking, or writing, or cement work or … you name it. Anytime you can put your own flair into something that you are doing, you release a little bit of that creative side. It's good for you.

You only have one life on earth. You have things you want to do. You don't want to *leave any life on the table*. When we get sick (which happens to all of us) then we spend some of our precious time getting healthy. We need to try to keep this at a minimum. If you want to maximize your contribution and do as much as possible, you must be healthy. Spiritually, mentally, and physically.

Chapter 21

Learn and Grow

*Life is full of challenges. How you handle these
challenges is what builds character.*

— Erin Brockovich

Growing.

Nothing stays the same. If you are not growing, you're going
backwards. So put the time and effort into growing. Try new
things, make decisions, ask questions. These are all ways in
which we can continue to grow.

Work

Ideally, we move forward from a first time job making
minimum wage to a slightly better job making slightly more
money to a slightly better job making slightly more money
right on up the line until we are doing a job we love for a
company we care about with people who listen to us and
appreciate what we can give them.

*"Now, the way it works shipboard is, you do your
job. You do it good, you get a better job. Maybe you
get promoted from swab to mate"*

— Captain Ron, *Captain Ron*

Jim Rohn used to say that the best way to <u>move ahead</u> is to make yourself more valuable. The best way to make <u>more money</u> is to make yourself more valuable. Do the very best job you can at every job you have and your employer will see your value. If they don't then someone else will see your value and you will get your promotion or raises from someone else. The more valuable you are the more money you will make. Are there people that make incredibly huge sums? Yes there are. Do they deserve it? Neither you nor I can say that for certain, but if the work a woman does makes her company $100 million, isn't it worth it to them to pay her $50 million? Let's not be jealous of what other people have accomplished, let's continue to make ourselves more valuable. There is absolutely no reason that you cannot be one of those people that makes $100 million a year.

The key to improving your value is through growing. We grow through education by learning new things, by studying, by attending seminars, by listening to speeches, by reading books, by getting help from professionals. We learn by doing a job and doing it well and by making mistakes at that job. We've learned new stuff by everything that we do, if we examine it afterwards.

One way that we can grow, which many people miss, is by asking for help. No one knows everything. The only way to learn everything is to ask others to help us learn it. We'll never get there but it is a fun goal to think about. Look for mentors, people who have done what you are trying to do and try to emulate them. What worked for them and what didn't work for them? There will be some things that worked for them that won't work for you, but you won't know that until you try it. Again keep in mind you must stay consistent with your beliefs and values.

Read

Reading will do more for your mind than anything else. You can learn anything you want to learn. An entire World History is available to you. Millions of people have put lessons out there for you to learn from. God Himself gave you a collection of books to read.

Exercise

Get out there and do stuff. Move those muscles and bones around. The more you use them, the more you will be able to use them, and the longer you will be able to use them. If you spend all your time sitting in a recliner, you will eventually become a lazy boy, unable to do stuff. Keep building your body.

Decision-Making

Is it a gut feeling or facts? I believe both can be valid. I think "gut feelings" come from details that we have subconsciously evaluated.

So, to make a decision we gather information, compare that to our principles (never go against them), our roles, our skills, and our goals.

Then decide.

A lot of people miss the "decide" part or just can't choose. Sometimes it is fear of making a wrong decision that prevents one from being made. If you have researched and compared them to your principles and priorities, then you won't make a BAD decision. You will have eliminated those.

Will you pick the best one? No one will ever know for sure. You will most likely pick a good one. Just pick one and roll with it.

Sometimes we subconsciously know which decision is our preferred, but we can't bring it to the surface. One trick that has worked for me is to flip a coin. Assign one decision to heads and the other to tails. So, "Choice A" is heads and "Choice B" is tails. Then I flip the coin. If heads comes up, and I am glad, then I do "A," if I am disappointed, then I choose" B." If I'm neither happy or disappointed, then I follow the coin toss.

This helps me.

We learn through every decision we make, if we take the time to examine them. What was the result of the decision? What could have made it better? What did I forget to look at? When we decide something, we learn about the topic, but we also get better at deciding things!

Decision-Making Part 2—Take the Money Out

When trying to make an ethical decision, I have found that usually money is involved. If money isn't in the picture, most people have no real problems seeing right and wrong. They are pretty instinctive about how the question stacks up against their values. But as soon as money gets in the picture, it gets cloudier. If someone offers us a $1,000,000, we can forget to check our own standards of right and wrong. Perhaps out of pure excitement.

If you find yourself trying to make an ethical decision, ask yourself what decision you would make if money was not part of it. You have to be honest with yourself on the answer. This may help you to see your right and wrong a little clearer

Other People

Other people complicate our lives. We complicate theirs too, so it's fair.

One thing that can ease some of the tension is to evaluate how your actions will affect others. Will someone have to do more work because you did or didn't do something? Will they feel worse about themselves because of you, or will they feel better?

Respect their time, arrive when you say you will, start and end meetings on time, and learn the rules of the road/game/ event so you can act within them.

It's straightforward. It just takes a little thought and a little effort.

You can do this.

Learn from your mistakes

We all make mistakes. Most of the stuff I know I learned from doing something wrong.

I have a motorcycle. I enjoy it. If you have one, make sure you take a safety course, and remember what they teach you.

I have a 1982 Honda Nighthawk 750. It's the kind of motorcycle that looks like a traditional motorcycle. Black with red striping. Classic.

I was visiting a friend of mine who also rode. When it came time for me to leave, I didn't resist the urge to show off a little bit, so I accelerated a little quicker than I should have.

Now I can't say for certain that I did a wheelie, but I can tell you that I almost flew off the back of the bike. I held it together and made it safely home. I also learned a lesson about how to safely get a motorcycle moving. You see, even I can learn from my mistakes.

Section V
Final Remarks

I'm writing this as I sit beside my mother's grave. She was taken from us way too soon. I've already had more time on this Earth than she did. I think this is an appropriate place to write this because it illustrates very clearly that we don't know how much time we have.

And there are a few things that I want to make sure that you know. Whoever you are.

First—**You MATTER.**

If you don't take anything else from this book, I hope you take this. You matter.

There has never been anyone else exactly like you and there never will be. The thoughts and perspectives that you can share, no one else can. There are people who need to hear what you have to share; and they will only hear *you*. No one else. You have a combination of gifts and talents and information that is uniquely you—that no one else can share. We need you.

Second—**Hard Times.**

You are going to have hard times. Things won't always go the way you want them to or think you need them to. But tough times don't last forever. You have the strength and the knowledge to get through it.

Some days I found faith meant just tying my shoes.

— Billy Sprague

You will go through times when getting out of bed will take all the strength you have. You can do it. Tie your shoes, take one step, and then another. Eventually, you will have found your way through.

Third—**You Need Others.**

There are people out there who are just as weird as you. Find them. Get to know them. Lean on them and let them lean on you.

Celebrate the joyous occasions of this life together. As the old saying goes 'a trouble shared is halved and a joy shared is doubled.'

Find those people. If they wrong you, patch it up. If you wrong them, patch it up. If either of you refuses, then you both lose.

Fourth—**Build the Best You.**

This book doesn't have all the answers. It is my hope that it will help you to find them. The first thing you need to do is the hardest—and you've probably already done it. I know because you made it to the end of this book.

Make the decision to find and build the best life possible. The life that God wants for you and will help you to build.

Next, you figure out who you are and what and who is important to you.

Then, you create your 'perfect life' in your mind and make the plan to build it.

Then, you get to work.

You will change as you go through your life, but that's good. If you are growing, you are changing.

It is my prayer for you that you will find the joy of purpose, and the joy of serving others, and that you will build an amazing life …

… and on your final breath you will think "What a ride! That was great. And I didn't leave any life on the table."

Appendix

Brainstorming

Brainstorming is for getting ideas out of your brain. Not for evaluation. I have used all of these at different times. You will see as you look at these examples from the creation of this book that not all of the ideas written in the brainstorm made it into the book. There are also things in the book that weren't on the brainstorm. It's a process. Let it go where it goes.

Cloud Brainstorming

The image here is a cloud brainstorm for the writing of this book. It starts with a central circle, in this case LLOT (Leaving Life on the Table). Major ideas branch out from it and ideas related to those ideas branch out from them. Just write them down where they belong. If they don't fit anywhere, just write it on the side and add it to a branch that shows up if appropriate, or perhaps it is the start of a new branch.

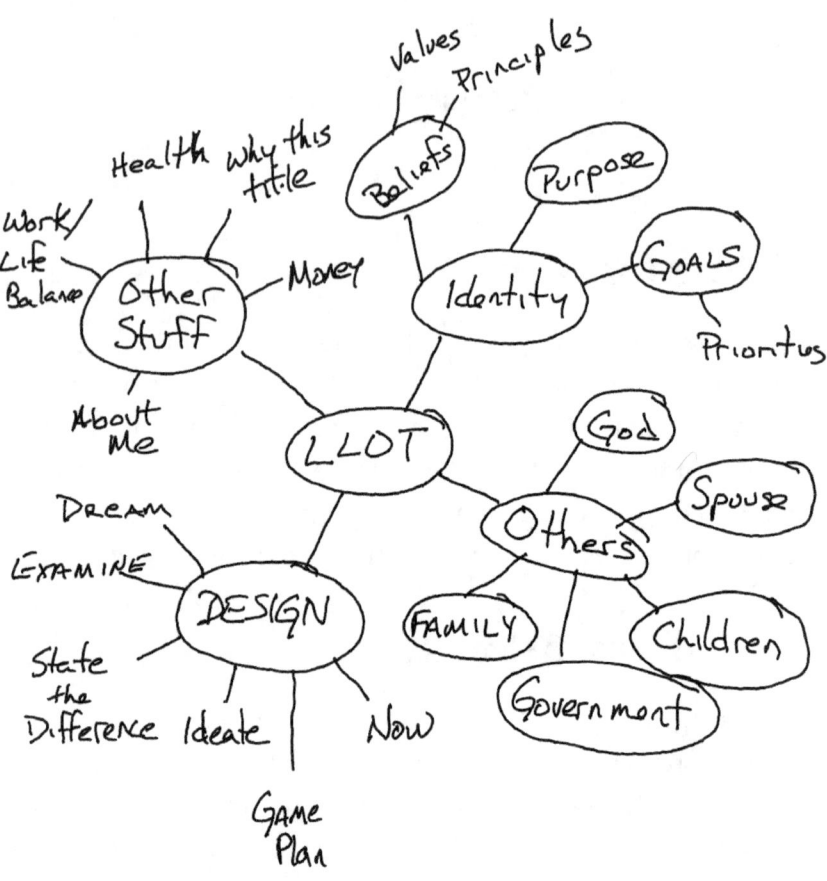

List Brainstorming

List Brainstorming appears a bit more organized. You write down your main points, then you write down the ideas that fit under them. Every time you have a new point that has subpoints, you make a new list.

L.L.O.T.

Who Am I

Beliefs
Values
Principles

DESIGN

Dream
Examine
State the Diff
Ideate
Game Plan
Now

What Do I Want?

Goals
What is important
What is success

Others/ Communication

God
Spouse
Kids
Parents
Extended
Government
Friends

Free-flow brainstorming

Free-flow brainstorming is just writing down things as you think of them. No organization at all. You just write down the ideas as they come to you. This is the truest form of brainstorming. I typically will use this method first and then go to either cloud or list to organize and brainstorm a bit more on certain topics.

L.L.O.T.

Purpose

Spouse

Goals

Core Values — Priorities

God

Friends

DESIGN

Money

Health

FAMILY

Time

Budgeting

Exercise

Diet

Step-by-Step

Worksheets are available in the appendix or at www.theCoach.vip/SLLOT

1. Write out as many beliefs as you can.

2. Carefully choose the best words to describe your beliefs.

3. Choose which beliefs are most important to your life, these are values.

4. Write down some principles that come from the values.

5. Ask yourself the questions presented in the chapter and write down the answers.

6. Ask others the questions presented in the chapter and write down the answers.

7. Organize the answers and look for patterns.

8. List as many of your roles as makes sense to you.

9. Write down any thoughts you have about why they are important to you.

10. Identify the 10 roles that are most important to you and why. Get a general idea of their priority for you. Number them if you can. Put them in that order.

11. Describe what success looks like to you.

12. Who is your God or your driving force?

13. What are some ways you can get to know God or your truth better?

14. What are some things you can do, that you are not already doing, to improve your relationship with your spouse? Write them down.

15. Ask your spouse to tell you about their goals and dreams. Use your new listening skills.

16. Are there any relationships that are in your top 10 priorities that are not as smooth as you wish they were? How might you address it?

17. Are there any associations in your life that are bad for you? What can you do about it?

18. Dream. Picture that perfect life and write down the details.

19. List major categories and what your dream is like in those categories.

20. Examine. Do you have a current state listed for every dream listed?

21. State the differences between the future and the present.

22. Generate as many ideas as possible to bridge the gap between now and future.

23. Game Plan. Choose the steps to get from 'now' to 'dream.' Especially the first step.

24. Repeat steps 19–21 for every dream.

25. Now, Do it! Start now with step 1.

Beliefs, Values and Principles

What do I believe?

Purpose

Why do I exist?

John@theCoach.vip   www.theCoach.vip

Roles

What roles do I fill?

What are my roles?	What are my highest priority roles?	Why is this role important to me?

Goals

What are some of the Goals in my life?

Dream

No restrictions. Describe this area of your life if it were perfect. What are you doing, how does it feel, who else is involved, why are you doing it

Area of concern	Dream
What area of your life are you focusing on?	*Organize the dreams into particular areas of your life. Do they match a role or a task or a goal?*

Area of focus	Examine
What area of your life are you focusing on?	Within this area, list what currently exists in your life. How does it feel, what do you like, what don't you like?

Specific traits

*List out the areas of your Dreams
and the areas of Examine.*

State the Difference

*What is different between your
present situation and your future dream?*

Specific traits	**Ideate**
List the specific items that are different between now and later	What are all the different ways you could get from now to then? No restrictions, no idea is too weird. Use a separate page for each difference.

Specific traits	Game Plan
List the specific items that are different between now and later	Using the ideas you came up with in the previous step, choose the one you think will serve you best. It should be consistent with your goals and beliefs. List all of the required steps that you will undertake.

Specific Game Plan

List the steps required to get from A > B

Now

When will you do them? Step #1 will be your exact start date. The remaining steps will be approximate.

About the Author

JOHN T. SALZWEDEL worked in the insurance industry for more than 25 years. He has served in leadership positions in both non-profit and for-profit organizations. Shortly after his fiftieth birthday, he felt the pull of a different purpose.

John was trained and certified by the John Maxwell Team and the Dave Ramsey Organization to be a life coach, speaker, and personal finance coach. He is an award-winning speaker, has earned a bachelor's degree in business, and a master's degree in management.

When he isn't working you might find John in his woodshop, collecting coins, volunteering with Ottawa County Emergency Services, teaching his dog, Dapple tricks and agility, or exploring the outdoors.

John has two children and two grandchildren by blood and many more of each by "life." He was born in Columbus, Wisconsin, and now lives in West Michigan with his wife, Susan and their two dogs, Dapple and Emmett.